Kari — S...
Mary — D

Who does Jesus say He is? This interactive exploration of the identity statements Jesus makes in John's gospel will encourage and strengthen the faith of Christians. It will also help deepen the reader's appreciation for the Bible-wide scope which demonstrates how Jesus is the Yes! to every Old Testament promise. This accessible study could be used for personal study or in small group formats. I highly recommend this thoughtfully designed resource to you!

DONALD C. GUTHRIE
Professor of Educational Ministries
Trinity Evangelical Divinity School

I have seen Becky Kiern's love for Jesus, His kingdom, and His word on display from her days as a college student . . . And those loves have only grown . . . Becky brings you near to the heart of God in the heart of Jesus in this study on the "I Am" statements of our Lord. Come journey with Becky through the "I Am's" of Jesus and discover your own identity in fresh and deeper ways in the person and work of Jesus.

PAUL HAHN
Coordinator, Mission to North America
Presbyterian Church in America (PCA)

This curriculum uses multiple methods to engage us in deep study of gospel passages in light of the whole Bible and God's redemptive story. Then, each lesson helps us respond anew to Jesus's words in our daily lives. As a master educator, Kiern leads us not only to understand a passage well, but also to learn *how* to study the Bible better in general. Unique strengths include the printed Bible passages with lots of space for marking observations on the text and the carefully worded questions to promote meaningful group discussion.

TASHA CHAPMAN, PHD
Professor of Educational Ministries
Covenant Theological Seminary

We live in a culture that entices individuals to curate their identities around paper-thin temporal façades. *Our Light and Life: Identity in the Claims of Christ* is an accessible Bible study that will have you referencing eternal truths from cover to cover. Its contents reflect upon the beautiful portraits of the I AM and remind us that He is our only reference point to figure out who we were truly made to be.

KAREN HODGE
CDM's Coordinator of Women's Ministries for the Presbyterian Church in America (PCA)
Author of *Transformed: Life-taker to Life-giver* and *Life-giving Leadership*

The invisible God has revealed Himself to us through His Son, Jesus. But who did Jesus claim to be? How did He describe Himself to us? *Our Light and Life* is an excellent resource for diving deep into the seven "I Am" statements of Jesus. To answer these questions, Kiern takes us not only to the Gospel of John but also back into the Old Testament. She shows us the significance of these statements and reminds us that Jesus truly is the fulfillment of all the promises of God. This study is rich and accessible, making it perfect for individual time in the Word as well as a helpful guide for group discussions.

ABBY ROSS HUTTO
Director of Spiritual Formation
Story Presbyterian Church, Westerville, Ohio
Author of *God for Us: Discovering the Heart of the Father through the Life of the Son*

Clear, concise, and deep—this is one of the most helpful resources for the personal study of Jesus's "I Am" statements in John. If you are looking for something to guide you through who Jesus is, and who you are because of Him, search no further.

SIMON STOKES
Reformed University Fellowship
University of North Carolina

The Christian subculture is cluttered with books and studies that pivot around the author or the reader. *Our Light and Life* resists this trend and encourages readers to begin and end with Scripture, and to stay close to the text when applying it to their lives. Using a mix of Bible study techniques, Becky Kiern ties Jesus's "I Am" statements into the warp and woof of redemptive history—from Genesis to Revelation—to remind readers of their own identity in Christ.

PATRICK J. O'BANION
International Trainer
Training Leaders International

Using the searchlight of Jesus's "I Am" statements in the Gospel of John, Becky Kiern's *Our Light and Life: Identity in the Claims of Christ* guides us to see Him and ourselves with new clarity and depth. Old Testament background coupled with New Testament continuity and fulfillment in Christ lead us to see the big story of Scripture and our part in it. With searching questions that faithfully employ biblical study tools, individuals and groups who seriously engage with the Scriptures through this study cannot help but grow in their knowledge and love of the Savior.

MARY BETH MCGREEVY
Adjunct Professor, Covenant Theological Seminary
Retreat and Conference Speaker

I am grateful for this study Becky has prepared on the "I Am" statements of Jesus in John. She combines pertinent textual comments, insightful reflection questions, important cross references, and penetrating applications, all with a warm, encouraging style. She has made a real contribution to help all of us engage in these vital passages of Scripture.

BOB BURNS, PHD
Pastor of Spiritual Formation
Church of the Good Shepherd, Durham, NC

Our Light and Life guides participants in exploring the depth and significance of Jesus's "I Am" statements. Through interacting with the biblical and cultural context of Jesus's words, we're invited to reflect on how they speak to our hearts now. This study is rich, accessible, and engaging, and will equip and encourage participants to know and love Jesus more.

JENILYN SWETT, MDIV.
Director of Adult Ministries
Restoration Community Church
St. Louis, Missouri

This study is jam-packed with Scripture as well as insightful questions! I'm thankful for a resource that offers more than knowledge; it offers an understanding of God and His love for us.

SUSAN TYNER
Trinity Presbyterian Church
Fort Worth, TX

What Becky Kiern has brought to life about our identity and hope in Jesus is phenomenal. This study is practical, rich with biblical content, and offers great Hope that Jesus is who He says He is, and we can find respite in Him.

CASEY COCKRUM, MS
Director of Campus Staff
Reformed University Fellowship

Presbyterian Church in America
DISCIPLESHIP MINISTRIES
1700 North Brown Road | Suite 102 | Lawrenceville, Georgia 30043
www.pcabookstore.com | 1.800.283.1357

Published by:
Committee on Discipleship Ministries
1700 North Brown Road, Suite 102
Lawrenceville, Georgia 30043
Bookstore: 1-800-283-1357
www.pcacdm.org/bookstore

ISBN: 978-1-944964-50-4
Designer: Jason Jung

Our Light and Life:

IDENTITY IN THE CLAIMS OF CHRIST

Becky Kiern

"In Him was life, and the life was the light of men. The light shines in the darkness, and the darkness has not overcome it."

JOHN 1:4-5

To my family, friends, professors and pastors: your love and encouragement support me as I cultivate my passions. To the women who allow me into their lives as a Bible teacher: your trust pushes me to keep fumbling towards faithfulness.

To James, Naomi, Judah and Ethan: you have been the best form of procrastination an aunt could ask for. May you always be rooted in the Lord's unfailing love—your true identity.

Our Light and Life:

IDENTITY IN THE CLAIMS OF CHRIST

INTRODUCTION

Some of my most treasured childhood memories are of the post-dinner stories my grandfather would tell. Most of the time he was a man of few words, but after he finished eating, his chair would be pushed back, his fingers would link together, and his hands would rest on top of his post-retirement pot belly. As a smile spread across his face, he would look at us and ask, "Did I ever tell you about the time . . ." Through his stories we were transported back to 1940s Jackson Square, to the French Quarter beignet shop where men in tuxes and women in ballgowns dropped white sugar all over their carnival attire. We were taken on grand adventures, sleeping under picnic tables while hiking the rim of the Grand Canyon and working odd jobs on the home front while the older family and friends fought across Europe and the Pacific. It has been fifteen years since I have heard him tell a story or seen his full-bellied laugh, but I can remember those precious moments like they were yesterday. Those stories taught me my family history, and later in life his stories helped me understand parts of who I am.

The other formative stories I remember as a child are the Bible stories told to me by the teachers and preachers I was privileged to have in my life. But even though I grew up reading the Bible, for a long time I saw it mostly as a well-collected group of stories, rules, and the occasional bit of poetry.

I believed then as I believe now that the Bible is infallible, God-inspired and true, but I did not see much cohesiveness. Thankfully, important roots began to grow in 2008 when I read through the Bible from cover to cover for the first time. As I read and studied, I began to see the cohesiveness and consistency of God's story.

In the fall of 2011, I was a new seminary graduate and a year into working my first women's ministry job. As I was planning our spring Bible study and trying to lay a historical redemptive foundation in our ministry, I decided the book of John would be a good place to begin. From the beginning of his book, John's goal was for his reader to believe that Jesus is the main part of God's cohesive plan of redemption. I didn't know it at the time, but as I prepared and taught the material, the journey towards writing this study had begun. Over the years that followed I would go on to teach Jesus's "I Am" statements in Bible studies and women's retreats across a variety of states. Each time I prepared and taught the material, it would grow—and praise the Lord!—I would grow with it.

It is commonly said the beauty of the Gospel of John is that while it is theologically deep, it is simple enough for first-time Bible readers to gather rich truth. I think this comes in part because John was a master storyteller. As he wove together poetry, metaphors, narrative and theological teaching,

John transported his readers back to the 30s A.D., to places like the streets of Jerusalem or a hillside in Galilee. And as John recounted the stories of his time with Jesus, he invited his reader into a deeper understanding of God's consistent, caring, covenantal relationship with His people. Through my grandfather's stories I grew to understand my family identity. Through John's writing I have grown to understand my core identity: a daughter of the king, called, redeemed, and united to Christ. I pray this study provides a helpful guide through Jesus's identity claims as you grow in belief and in a deeper understanding of your identity in Christ.

HOW TO USE THIS STUDY

Our Light and Life is an inductive Bible study designed to help you spend the bulk of your devotional time in the Word of God. The scripture passages quoted all come from the English Standard Version, and while you don't have to use this translation, make sure you have a Bible in your hand every time you sit down.

Growing in Wisdom and Skill

This study is written with two main purposes. The first is to help you cultivate a growing relationship with the Lord through studying His Word (Ps. 119:169-176; Prov. 3:1-3; 2 Tim. 3:14-17). The writer of Hebrews encouraged readers to engage with the Bible: "for the word of God is living and active, sharper than any two-edged sword, piercing to the division of soul and of spirit, of joints and of marrow, and discerning the thoughts and intentions of the heart" (Heb. 4:12). God's Word is true, trustworthy, and transformative, so dive into each text given, read it, mark it up, and engage in asking it good questions.

Second, this study is formatted to encourage you in developing the skill of biblical study. Knowing how to study the Bible is the most important tool a Christian can acquire. When you read a passage, begin by asking what it says about God and His work before you attempt to apply it to your own life. *Our Light and Life* was written to help you grow in this process. Each chapter has been designed to help you carefully study selected passages by working through the steps of observation, analysis, and application. Each step in this method is labeled:

THINK ABOUT IT – An introduction to the lesson to help you think on the topic before digging into the text

WHAT DO YOU SEE? – Observation: What is in the text?

WHAT DO YOU THINK? – Analysis: What does the text teach about God and His story?

WHAT'S IT TO YOU? – Application: What does the text teach us about ourselves in the light of God, and how can we use it in our lives?

Historical-Redemptive Bible Study

The Historical-Redemptive view of Scripture is a way of interpreting the Bible in which all of history, from before the creation of the world to the ushering in of the new creation and beyond, is telling the story of God's faithful redemption of His people. It teaches the biblical storyline of creation, rebellion, redemption, and restoration. In other words,

- God made a good creation;

- Rebellion (sin) entered into the story;

- God sent Jesus as a faithful sacrifice to redeem mankind; and

- God is actively working until the day He restores all things.

This study focuses on the identity statements Christ made about Himself which are recorded in the Gospel of John. Each "I Am" statement from John's gospel is broken into two studies: the first week you will study the Old Testament passages to which Jesus is referring; the second week you will study the context of Jesus's teaching. The study culminates with Jesus's final "I Am" statement from Revelation. Looking back at the work of God, then to the teaching and work of Jesus, and finally looking forward to the things to come will reveal the thread of God's covenant promises throughout history.

The Indicative Instructs the Imperative

Writing a study on cultivating your identity can quickly get off course if either the writer or the reader mixes up the indicatives and imperatives of Scripture. So, what are they, and why do they matter so much?

The indicative is the truth of what God has done and of who we are in Christ, while the imperative instructs us how we should therefore live. For example:

Deuteronomy 5:6-21: "I am the Lord your God, who brought you out of the land of Egypt, out of the house of slavery." (indicatives)
[Therefore] "You shall . . ." (imperative)
John 15:1-4: "I am the vine." (indicative)
[Therefore] "Abide in Me." (imperative)

From Genesis to Revelation the whole Bible is telling the story of God's divine actions (His indicatives) and how His people should therefore live (imperatives). Thus, when looking at any passage in Scripture you should ask, "What is God's indicative action, and therefore, what is my imperative response?" As Christians our identity (who we are and what we should do) is always based in the work that the Lord has already done.

"Nearly all the wisdom we possess, that is to say, true and sound wisdom, consists of two parts: the knowledge of God and of ourselves. . . Yet, however the knowledge of God and of ourselves may be mutually connected, the order of right teaching requires that we discuss the former first, then proceed afterward to treat the latter."

JOHN CALVIN[1]

The Knowledge of God and of Ourselves

"Therefore, My people shall know My name. Therefore, in that day they shall know that it is I who speak; here I am."

ISAIAH 52:6

THINK ABOUT IT

Do you find the question, "Who am I?" difficult to answer? Why is this a difficult question to answer?

Who Am I?

"Who am I?"—Is there a question more central or universal to the human experience? These three little words, this tiny question, can take a lifetime to unravel. For generations, poets, songwriters, sociologists, and anthropologists (just to name a few) have attempted to romanticize or research their way to a deeper understanding of human and personal identity. For the Christian, the question is also warranted. God invites His people to freely ask identity questions, knowing in His kindness He has already given them the answers in His Word.

As readers enter into God's Word, as they begin to digest God's divinity, His story and promises, they are invited to understand the fundamental truth: there is no real knowledge of self without a knowledge of God. And at the core we cannot truly answer the question "Who am I?" until we have answered, "Who is He?"

So, who is God? The four gospel books were written to help the Church know and understand the person and work of Jesus Christ. But the Gospel of John is different from the other three books (the Synoptic Gospels: Matthew, Mark, and Luke) in that John writes his book not simply to recount Jesus's life, but to help explain Jesus's identity and unique relationship with God the Father.

John, an ethnic and religious Jew, originally wrote his book for both a Jewish and non-Jewish audience. Having been raised in the synagogue studying the Torah and the other scriptural texts, John recognized the thread of God's covenant promises running throughout Jesus's teaching. In his book, he wanted to make it abundantly clear to others that Jesus is the Son of God who came to fulfill the promises of God the Father. Or as John puts it, "these are written so that you may believe that Jesus is the Christ, the Son of God, and that by believing you may have life in His name" (John 20:31). In His name is found identity and life. But what is His name and who is He?

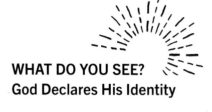

WHAT DO YOU SEE?
God Declares His Identity

Read and mark the following passages from Exodus.

- Circle the participants in these narrative passages.

- Highlight identification statements God made about Himself.

- Highlight Moses's fears.

- In yet another color, highlight God's promises.

- In the margin make note of how God wants to be remembered.

Exodus 3:9-15

⁹And now, behold, the cry of the people of Israel has come to Me, and I have also seen the oppression with which the Egyptians oppress them. ¹⁰Come, I will send you to Pharaoh that you may bring My people, the children of Israel, out of Egypt." ¹¹But Moses said to God, "Who am I that I should go to Pharaoh and bring the

children of Israel out of Egypt?"
[12]He said, "But I will be with
you, and this shall be the sign
for you, that I have sent you:
when you have brought the
people out of Egypt, you shall
serve God on this mountain."

[13]Then Moses said to God, "If I
come to the people of Israel and
say to them, 'The God of your
fathers has sent me to you,' and
they ask me, 'What is His name?'
what shall I say to them?" [14]God
said to Moses, "I AM WHO I
AM." And He said, "Say this to
the people of Israel: 'I AM has
sent me to you.'" [15]God also
said to Moses, "Say this to the
people of Israel: 'The LORD, the
God of your fathers, the God of
Abraham, the God of Isaac, and
the God of Jacob, has sent me
to you.' This is My name forever,
and thus I am to be remembered
throughout all generations."

Exodus 5:22-6:5

[22]Then Moses turned to the

LORD and said, "O Lord, why have You done evil to this people? Why did You ever send me? [23]For since I came to Pharaoh to speak in Your name, he has done evil to this people, and You have not delivered Your people at all."

[6:1]But the LORD said to Moses, "Now you shall see what I will do to Pharaoh; for with a strong hand he will send them out, and with a strong hand he will drive them out of his land." [2]God spoke to Moses and said to him, "I am the LORD. [3]I appeared to Abraham, to Isaac, and to Jacob, as God Almighty, but by My name the LORD I did not make Myself known to them. [4]I also established My covenant with them to give them the land of Canaan, the land in which they lived as sojourners. [5]Moreover, I have heard the groaning of the people of Israel whom the Egyptians hold as slaves, and I have remembered My covenant."

1 In Exodus 3:11 and 13, Moses expressed doubt in his ability to do what God was asking him to do.

a. How did God respond to Moses's question?

I am—

b. Why might God have responded to Moses's question with declarations about His own identity?

assurance — He can do anything!

2 List the three names God gave to Moses in both passages as proof of His relationship with the people of Israel?

God of your fathers

3 In Exodus 6, God stated that He "established" and "remembered" His covenant.[2] Using a dictionary, look up and write out the definition of a covenant.

Covenant :- an agreement.

WHAT DO YOU THINK?
The Great I AM

When trying to understand a topic discussed in a passage of Scripture, it can be helpful to ask the questions "What do other passages say on this topic?" and "What does the whole Bible say about it?" Looking at other passages (known as referencing) is a helpful tool in analyzing a particular passage because it helps us understand connections made throughout the entire Bible.

God declared His identity in Exodus, but as God's story progressed, He continued to remind His people of His identity by making similar declarations throughout Scripture. So, generations after the exodus, God gave the prophet Isaiah a special revelation to share with His people.

4 God declared His identity multiple times throughout Isaiah. Read each passage given, using the charts to answer questions for each passage.

Who does God declare Himself to be?

ISAIAH
44:6-8

first + Last — No other Rock.

ISAIAH
48:17

Redeemer, Holy One of Israel, Lord your God.

ISAIAH
52:1-10

Sovereign, God of Israel

What does God promise to do?

ISAIAH
44:6-8

Proclaim my promises

ISAIAH
48:17

Teaches what is good — leads along paths

ISAIAH
52:1-10

Redeem us. Reveal His name, comforted us, demonstrated His power

To whom is God making promises?

ISAIAH
44:6-8

My witnesses

ISAIAH
48:17

The Redeemed.

ISAIAH
52:1-10

Zion, Jerusalem, My people

How are God's promises here similar to the promises given in the Exodus passages?

ISAIAH
44:6-8

Established a people

ISAIAH
48:17

Teaches us what is good., leads

ISAIAH
52:1-10

Redeemed, power demonstrated.

5 Isaiah was written as a guide to faithful, God-centered living, based on the covenant promises of God. List three ways God's declarative statements in Exodus and Isaiah are still true.

① He teaches what is good
② Redeemed us
③ Promises

6 How are the truths you listed in question 5 helpful in your own identity formation?

all things are good through christ

WHAT'S IT TO YOU?

7 Why do you think it is important to ask and try to answer the questions "Who am I?" and "Who is God?"

Our identity n christ.

8 Ask yourself, "Who am I?" Write out your answer.

Beloved of Christ

9 What are some other Bible passages that help you answer "Who am I"?

10 List some of the beliefs, relationships, or experiences in your life which have been a part of your attempts to cultivate your own identity? (Think of examples which have been both positive and negative.)

The Bible is one continuous story of God's redemptive love for His people. Studying Jesus's "I Am" statements in relationship to the Old Testament passages to which they correspond, helps reveal the steadfast identity of God. As the author of Hebrews wrote, "Jesus Christ is the same yesterday and today and forever" (Heb. 13:8).

11 In closing, take some time to pray and to journal. What comfort or frustration do you have in the knowledge that you can only know who you are in light of who God is?

Need to devote time.

The Bread of Life:
GOD'S CONTINUED FAITHFULNESS

"Truly, truly, I say to you, whoever believes has eternal life. I am the bread of life."

JOHN 6:47-48

THINK ABOUT IT

In the passages from Exodus and Isaiah in the last chapter, you saw some of the ways God declared His identity to Israel. Why do you think it is hard to believe God's promises even when He has given direct declarations?

Other factors? Not hearing Him?

Lost and Hungry

The Lord's provision for His people did not begin with Jesus's incarnation. Since the beginning, God had been protecting, providing, and working to restore His people. Before looking at the Gospel of John, return to Moses and the Israelites, to one of the many times they called out for the Lord's provision and He responded.

WHAT DO YOU SEE?
God Feeds the Israelites

1 Read Exodus 16:1-30 and Numbers 11:4-5, 10-15, and 31-33. Then list your observations in the charts that follow.

The People's Complaint:

EXODUS 16:1-30	Wilderness— starvation.
NUMBERS 11:4-5, 10-15, 31-33	Food, Meat

God's Response:

EXODUS
16:1-30

Heard + provided.

NUMBERS
11:4-5, 10-
15, 31-33

The Lord heard
+ sent.

**The Response of Moses and/or the People
to God's Response:**

EXODUS
16:1-30

Didn't follow
initially, saw
consequences, then
did.

NUMBERS
11:4-5, 10-
15, 31-33

Questioned God,
then saw the
promise.

Deuteronomy is the last book of what is known as the Pentateuch or Torah (the first five books of the Bible written by Moses). Through retelling portions of Israel's history—including God's promises to the patriarchs (Abraham, Isaac, and Jacob), the lessons learned during the forty years in the desert, and reteaching important aspects of God's Law—Deuteronomy encourages its readers to remember the faithfulness of God towards His people. Moses presented the Israelites with the Law (including the Ten Commandments) and its interpretation in Deuteronomy 5-9.

Read Deuteronomy 8:1-4, 11-20, marking the passage as instructed.

- Underline any repeated words or phrases.

- Highlight the things the Lord commands His people to remember.

- In a different color highlight the various things the Lord provided for the Israelites.

- Circle the main source of life for mankind.

Deuteronomy 8:1-4, 11-20

¹"The whole commandment that I command you today you shall be careful to do, that you may live and multiply, and go in and possess the land that the LORD swore to give to your fathers. ²And you shall remember the

43

whole way that the LORD your God has led you these forty years in the wilderness, that He might humble you, testing you to know what was in your heart, whether you would keep His commandments or not. ³And He humbled you and let you hunger and fed you with manna, which you did not know, nor did your fathers know, that He might make you know that man does not live by bread alone, but man lives by every word that comes from the mouth of the LORD. ⁴Your clothing did not wear out on you and your foot did not swell these forty years."

¹¹"Take care lest you forget the LORD your God by not keeping His commandments and His rules and His statutes, which I command you today, ¹²lest, when you have eaten and are full and have built good houses and live in them, ¹³and when your herds and flocks multiply and your silver and gold is

multiplied and all that you have is multiplied, [14]then your heart be lifted up, and you forget the LORD your God, who brought you out of the land of Egypt, out of the house of slavery, [15]who led you through the great and terrifying wilderness, with its fiery serpents and scorpions and thirsty ground where there was no water, who brought you water out of the flinty rock, [16]who fed you in the wilderness with manna that your fathers did not know, that He might humble you and test you, to do you good in the end. [17]Beware lest you say in your heart, 'My power and the might of my hand have gotten me this wealth.' [18]You shall remember the LORD your God, for it is He who gives you power to get wealth, that He may confirm His covenant that He swore to your fathers, as it is this day. [19]And if you forget the LORD your God and go after other gods and serve them and worship them, I solemnly

What is my wilderness right now –

How has God provided for me in the wilderness

How is He testing for good in the end?

45

warn you today that you shall surely perish. ²⁰Like the nations that the LORD makes to perish before you, so shall you perish, because you would not obey the voice of the LORD your God."

2 In many passages in the Bible God asks His people to remember who He is. Why does God make this request? Make note of any other passages in Scripture that may come to mind.

Think about what He has promised + delivered.

3 List the things God said He did first, to and for the Israelites.

4 List the things God requested, as a response of gratitude and faithfulness, from the Israelites.

Jesus Feeds the Crowd

Read and mark John 6:1-13.

- Highlight expressions of doubt.
- Circle the reason Jesus questioned Philip.
- In another color highlight or underline the people's reaction to Jesus.

John 6:1-13

¹*After this Jesus went away to the other side of the Sea of Galilee, which is the Sea of Tiberias.* ²*And a large crowd was following Him, because they saw the signs that He was doing on the sick.* ³*Jesus went up on the mountain, and there He sat*

down with His disciples. ⁴Now
the Passover, the feast of the
Jews, was at hand. ⁵Lifting up
His eyes, then, and seeing that a
large crowd was coming toward
Him, Jesus said to Philip,
"Where are we to buy bread,
so that these people may eat?"
⁶He said this to test him, for He
Himself knew what He would
do. ⁷Philip answered Him, "Two
hundred denarii worth of bread
would not be enough for each of
them to get a little." ⁸One of His
disciples, Andrew, Simon Peter's
brother, said to Him, ⁹"There is
a boy here who has five barley
loaves and two fish, but what
are they for so many?" ¹⁰Jesus
said, "Have the people sit down."
Now there was much grass in
the place. So the men sat down,
about five thousand in number.
¹¹Jesus then took the loaves, and
when He had given thanks, He
distributed them to those who
were seated. So also the fish,
as much as they wanted. ¹²And
when they had eaten their fill,

He told His disciples, "Gather
up the leftover fragments, that
nothing may be lost." [13]So they
gathered them up and filled
twelve baskets with fragments
from the five barley loaves left
by those who had eaten.

5 What question did Jesus ask Philip? If Jesus already knew the answer, why did He ask Philip the question?

Where do we buy bread?

6 Jesus was teaching the same lesson to Philip in John 6 as the Lord taught the Israelites, in the Exodus 16, Numbers 11, and Deuteronomy 8 passages. In your own words, explain the lesson being taught.

In the impossible situation — our interpretation + solution are not enough — the Lord always provides!

Read and mark John 6:22-36.

- Highlight the crowd's words.

- In another color, highlight Jesus's responses (His words only).

- Underline any words and phrases repeated by Jesus.

- Underline what the crowds seemed to want.

- Circle the "I am" statement and in the margin explain what it means to you.

John 6:22-36

[22]*On the next day the crowd that remained on the other side of the sea saw that there had been only one boat there, and that Jesus had not entered the boat with His disciples, but that His disciples had gone away alone.* [23]*Other boats from Tiberias came near the place where they had eaten the bread after the Lord had given thanks.* [24]*So when the crowd saw that Jesus was not there, nor His disciples, they themselves got into the boats and went to Capernaum, seeking Jesus.*

[25]When they found Him on the other side of the sea, they said to Him, "Rabbi, when did you come here?" [26]Jesus answered them, "Truly, truly, I say to you, you are seeking Me, not because you saw signs, but because you ate your fill of the loaves. [27]Do not work for the food that perishes, but for the food that endures to eternal life, which the Son of Man will give to you. For on Him God the Father has set His seal." [28]Then they said to Him, "What must we do, to be doing the works of God?" [29]Jesus answered them, "This is the work of God, that you believe in Him whom He has sent." [30]So they said to Him, "Then what sign do You do, that we may see and believe You? What work do You perform? [31]Our fathers ate the manna in the wilderness; as it is written, 'He gave them bread from heaven to eat.'" [32]Jesus then said to them, "Truly, truly, I say to you, it was not Moses who gave

you the bread from heaven, but My Father gives you the true bread from heaven. 33For the bread of God is He who comes down from heaven and gives life to the world." 34They said to Him, "Sir, give us this bread always." 35Jesus said to them, "I am the bread of life; whoever comes to Me shall not hunger, and whoever believes in Me shall never thirst. 36But I said to you that you have seen Me and yet do not believe."

WHAT DO YOU THINK?
The Bread of Life

7 After He fed the crowd, how did they initially identify Jesus?

JOHN
6:14

Prophet.

JOHN
6:15

their king.

JOHN
6:25

Rabbi

8 In your own words explain the difference in what the crowd wanted in John 6:14, 15, and 25, and in what Jesus was offering.

Military + Political Leader vs Spiritual Father.

9 In John 6:28, the crowd asked, "What must we do, to be doing the works of God?" Pretend you haven't read Jesus's response and honestly consider how you tend to answer this question in your own life. List your answer(s).

Just Believe

10 Reflecting on John 6:36, what are some ways in our own lives and in our churches that we misinterpret/misperceive Jesus and fail to discern His real character?

Can't see real results.

WHAT'S IT TO YOU?

In the passages from John's gospel we see Jesus teaching that neither barley loaves, fish, nor manna are God's ultimate provision for His people. From the beginning of the story, God's ultimate and eternal provision for His people has been His Son. The Lord miraculously provided meat and bread for the Israelites, and yet Psalm 78:32 tells us: "In spite of all this, they still sinned; despite His wonders, they did not believe." Similarly, the Lord miraculously provided meat and bread for the crowd in Galilee, and yet the next day they asked, "What sign do You do, that we may see and believe You?" (John 6:30).

11 All of God's story bends towards redemption, and all of Scripture tells the story of God's faithfulness to an unfaithful people. God provided manna in the wilderness, and Jesus provided fish and bread to the crowd, and yet both groups still struggled to trust in the Lord's faithfulness.

a. When life is hard and it feels like you are wandering, hungry in the wilderness, why is it important to remember God's faithfulness?

His promises are always true. — we must be patient + believe!

b. What are some areas in your life where you struggle to believe that God continues to be faithful?

Clear answers.

c. The crowd wanted a sign or another meal, but Jesus gave them something far greater—He gave them Himself. How does knowing Jesus's provision give you hope?

His way is always the best!

In Ephesians 1:17-18a, Paul wrote to encourage his readers by praying "that the God of our Lord Jesus Christ, the Father of glory, may give you the Spirit of wisdom and of revelation in the knowledge of Him, having the eyes of your hearts enlightened, that you may know what is the hope to which He has called you."

12 As you end this lesson, take time to ask the Lord to enlighten the eyes of your heart. Pray He will help you remember times when you have seen His faithfulness and provision in your life, and that in remembering, your faith will be strengthened.

What am I grateful for?

The Bread of Life:
OUR NOURISHMENT

"Truly, truly, I say to you, whoever believes has eternal life. I am the bread of life."

JOHN 6:47-48

THINK ABOUT IT

Psalm 78 recounts the story of the Hebrew people, explaining that even with all the visible works of the Lord, the Israelites were still short on faith. Verse 17 states, "Yet they sinned still more against Him, rebelling against the Most High in the desert." God's people have always struggled to trust in His provisions—even Christians aren't always satisfied. Be honest with yourself and God and list some of your complaints. (Don't worry, He can take it.) Pray openly about each and lay them before His throne. Note any response that may come to mind.

Not growing old w/ Rod,

WHAT DO YOU SEE?
The Word Became Flesh

1 Read John 1:1-14. What does John say about the Word in the following passages?

John 1:1 The Word was _____,

the Word was _____, and the

Word was _____.

John 1:2 The Word was _____.

John 1:3 _____ through the

Word, and without the Word _____.

John 1:4 In the Word was _____,

and it was _____.

John 1:14 The Word _____

and _____.

2 According to John 6:38-40, and from the verses above, who is the Word and what is the will of the Father?

WHAT DO YOU THINK?

Read and mark the following passages.

- Underline every reference to bread.

- Highlight any reference to life.

- In another color highlight any reference to death.

- Circle any "I am" statements.

- In the margins compare the types of bread discussed in the passages.

John 3:14-16, 36

[14]And as Moses lifted up the serpent in the wilderness, so must the Son of Man be lifted up, [15]that whoever believes in Him may have eternal life. [16]"For God so loved the world, that He gave his only Son, that whoever believes in Him should not perish but have eternal life.

[36]Whoever believes in the Son has eternal life; whoever does not obey the Son shall not see life, but the wrath of God remains on him.

John 5:24

[24]Truly, truly, I say to you, whoever hears My word and believes Him who sent Me has eternal life. He does not come into judgment, but has passed from death to life.

John 6:35-58

[35]Jesus said to them, "I am the bread of life; whoever comes to Me shall not hunger, and

whoever believes in Me shall never thirst. ³⁶But I said to you that you have seen Me and yet do not believe. ³⁷All that the Father gives Me will come to Me, and whoever comes to Me I will never cast out. ³⁸For I have come down from heaven, not to do My own will but the will of Him who sent Me. ³⁹And this is the will of Him who sent Me, that I should lose nothing of all that He has given Me, but raise it up on the last day. ⁴⁰For this is the will of My Father, that everyone who looks on the Son and believes in Him should have eternal life, and I will raise him up on the last day." ⁴¹So the Jews grumbled about Him, because He said, "I am the bread that came down from heaven." ⁴²They said, "Is not this Jesus, the son of Joseph, whose father and mother we know? How does He now say, 'I have come down from heaven'?" ⁴³Jesus answered them, "Do not grumble among yourselves. ⁴⁴No one can come

to Me unless the Father who
sent Me draws him. And I will
raise him up on the last day.
⁴⁵It is written in the Prophets,
'And they will all be taught by
God.' Everyone who has heard
and learned from the Father
comes to Me— ⁴⁶not that anyone
has seen the Father except He
who is from God; He has seen
the Father. ⁴⁷Truly, truly, I say
to you, whoever believes has
eternal life. ⁴⁸I am the bread
of life. ⁴⁹Your fathers ate the
manna in the wilderness, and
they died. ⁵⁰This is the bread
that comes down from heaven,
so that one may eat of it and
not die. ⁵¹I am the living bread
that came down from heaven. If
anyone eats of this bread, he will
live forever. And the bread that I
will give for the life of the world
is My flesh." ⁵²The Jews then
disputed among themselves,
saying, "How can this man give
us His flesh to eat?" ⁵³So Jesus
said to them, "Truly, truly, I say
to you, unless you eat the flesh

of the Son of Man and drink His blood, you have no life in you. ⁵⁴Whoever feeds on My flesh and drinks My blood has eternal life, and I will raise him up on the last day. ⁵⁵For my flesh is true food, and My blood is true drink. ⁵⁶Whoever feeds on My flesh and drinks My blood abides in Me, and I in him. ⁵⁷As vthe living Father sent Me, and I live because of the Father, so whoever feeds on Me, he also will live because of Me. ⁵⁸This is the bread that came down from heaven, not like the bread the fathers ate, and died.

3 John 1:14 tells us, "The Word became flesh and dwelt among us." From the passages you just read and marked, summarize in your own words: Why did the Word become flesh?

Feeding on the Word

The Bible is often described as the "word of God" because it is the primary way God has chosen to reveal His personhood and purposes to the world. But as Calvin explains, John called the Son of God "the Word" in the opening of his gospel, "because He is the eternal wisdom and will of God" and "the exact image of God's purpose."[3] In other words, we look to the Bible, the word, to know who God is and what He has done, and subsequently, we look to Jesus, the Word, to see God's wisdom, purpose, and will incarnate.

4 What is the metaphor Jesus used in John 6:53-58?

5 With your answer from question 4 in mind, what is Jesus teaching with His controversial statement in John 6:53-58? Why was it controversial in first century Israel, and how is it controversial today?

6 The passages in John tell us Jesus is the Word and the Living Bread. Use the chart that follows to discover how you can feed on Him in your own life today.

How are we instructed to feed upon the Word?

DEUTERONOMY
6:4-7

How are we instructed to feed upon the Word?

PSALM
1:1-4

PROVERBS
3:1-8

LUKE
22:14-20

1 CORINTHIANS
11:23-26

7 With all the passages studied in this lesson in mind, explain what you think Jesus meant when He stated, "I am the bread of life . . . I am the living bread that came down from heaven. If anyone eats of this bread, he will live forever. And the bread that I will give for the life of the world is My flesh" (John 6:48, 51).

WHAT'S IT TO YOU?

8 Often, we forget the extent to which we need God in our lives. By using the metaphor of food, Jesus is reminding us that relationship with Him is as necessary for our spiritual well-being as food is for our physical bodies. Often when we neglect our relationship with the Lord and attempt to live life through our own strength, we can notice signs of our unnourished hearts.

a. List any symptoms of spiritual malnourishment that are evident in your life. (e.g., being quick to anger over small offenses, anxiety, or cynical thoughts.)

b. When we are not being nourished by Christ, we are being fed by something else. We can be replacing Christ both with things that are seen as "good for you" (family, work, friends, working out) and with things which are "bad for you" (substance abuse, pornography, excessive retail therapy). List some of the things you rely upon for nourishment instead of Christ.

c. With the list you just made in mind, what are some ways you can receive nourishment from Christ?

9 Take a few moments to sit with the Lord. Remember His gifts of nourishment and life are just that, gifts. The Son of God "became flesh and dwelt among us" (John 1:14). He took on human form, lived a humble life, died a horrific death, and victoriously conquered death, because He loves being with you. He loves hearing your voice, and He loves feeding you rich truth through His Word. Ask Him to do just that today.

The Light of the World:
GOD'S PROMISED STEADFAST LOVE

"I am the light of the world. Whoever follows Me will not walk in darkness, but will have the light of life."

JOHN 8:12

THINK ABOUT IT

Light and dark are stark contradictions commonly used throughout Scripture, most often to illustrate life lived with or without the holiness of God. Similar to His use of bread to illustrate our need for God's provision, Jesus used this universally known concept of light for His next teaching point.

Why did Jesus choose ordinary things such as bread, light, or darkness to help illustrate His identity and explain complex truth? How do such illustrations help you understand His teachings?

WHAT DO YOU SEE?
Light and Dark in the Old Testament

Jesus taught that He is the Light of the world. On the surface, Jesus's teaching appears quite simple, but to the Jewish people, His words were a bold claim. Reading through the Old Testament reveals a people who were repeatedly rebelling against God and each other, sometimes in atrocious ways. Nevertheless, all of God's story is leading to redemption. Thus, while the Old Testament reveals a rebellious people, it more importantly reveals the power of God whose promised redemption cannot be stopped. Before getting into Jesus's teaching in John, take time to review some of the Old Testament passages which connect Jesus's identity statement to the larger story of God's relationship with His people.

A Description of Darkness

Often darkness is used in the Bible as a metaphor for a life lived without God.

Read and mark the following passages from Isaiah 59.

- Highlight the various descriptions of sin and darkness (e.g., iniquity, injustice).

- Mark words or phrases that are repeated.
- In the margins list at least three ways darkness is described in this passage.

Isaiah 59:1-4, 8-15

*¹Behold, the LORD's hand is not
shortened, that it cannot save,
or His ear dull, that it cannot
hear;
²but your iniquities have made a
separation
between you and your God,
and your sins have hidden His
face from you
so that He does not hear.
³For your hands are defiled with
blood
and your fingers with iniquity;
your lips have spoken lies;
your tongue mutters
wickedness.*

*⁸The way of peace they do not
know,
and there is no justice in their
paths;
they have made their roads
crooked;
no one who treads on them*

knows peace.
⁹Therefore justice is far from us,
and righteousness does not
overtake us;
we hope for light, and behold,
darkness,
and for brightness, but we walk
in gloom.
¹⁰We grope for the wall like the
blind;
we grope like those who have no
eyes;
we stumble at noon as in the
twilight,
among those in full vigor we are
like dead men.
¹¹We all growl like bears;
we moan and moan like doves;
we hope for justice, but there is
none;
for salvation, but it is far from
us.
¹²For our transgressions are
multiplied before You,
and our sins testify against us;
for our transgressions are with
us,
and we know our iniquities:
¹³transgressing, and denying

the LORD,
and turning back from following
our God,
speaking oppression and revolt,
conceiving and uttering from
the heart lying words.
14Justice is turned back,
and righteousness stands far
away;
for truth has stumbled in the
public squares,
and uprightness cannot enter.
15Truth is lacking,
and he who departs from evil
makes himself a prey.
The LORD saw it, and it
displeased Him
that there was no justice.
displeased Him that there was
no justice.

1 In this passage Isaiah was teaching the difference between God and His people. In your own words explain or rewrite Isaiah 59:1-2.

The Light Shines in the Darkness

Scripture often describes the darkness of our broken world, but more importantly, it prepares us for the coming dawn. It beckons us to remember the promises of God the Father, promises to provide eternal healing, reconciliation, and light through His Son Jesus.

A Description of Light

Just as darkness is a metaphor for life without God, light is often a metaphor for the holiness of God.

Read and mark the remainder of Isaiah 59, and then answer the questions provided.

- Highlight any references the passage makes to the Lord.

- In a different color highlight any repeated words or phrases.

- In the margins list three things that happen when God shines His holy light into darkness.

Isaiah 59:15b-21

[15b]*The LORD saw it, and it displeased Him that there was no justice.* [16]*He saw that there was no man, and wondered that there was no*

one to intercede;
then His own arm brought Him
salvation,
and His righteousness upheld
Him.
[17]He put on righteousness as a
breastplate,
and a helmet of salvation on His
head;
He put on garments of
vengeance for clothing,
and wrapped Himself in zeal as
a cloak.
[18]According to their deeds, so
will He repay,
wrath to His adversaries,
repayment to His enemies;
to the coastlands He will render
repayment.
[19]So they shall fear the name of
the LORD from the west,
and His glory from the rising of
the sun;
for He will come like a rushing
stream,
which the wind of the LORD
drives.
[20]"And a Redeemer will come to
Zion,

to those in Jacob who turn from
transgression," declares the
LORD.

[21] "And as for Me, this is My
covenant with them," says the
LORD: "My Spirit that is upon
you, and My words that I have
put in your mouth, shall not
depart out of your mouth, or out
of the mouth of your offspring,
or out of the mouth of your
children's offspring," says the
LORD, "from this time forth and
forevermore."

2 What promise does God make in Isaiah 59?

3 Read the following passages. For each passage identify two of the ways the author describes the Son of God and/or the work He will accomplish.

The Son of God Foretold

PSALM
36:5-11

ISAIAH
9:2, 6-7

ISAIAH
42:5-9

WHAT DO YOU THINK?

4 Isaiah 9:2 says, "The people who walked in darkness have seen a great light; those who dwelt in a land of deep darkness, on them has light shone." Take a moment to reflect. List some ways in which darkness seems to have more power than light.

5 Closely read either Psalm 27 or Psalm 36.

a. How might the psalmist's words help shine light into the dark places in your life?

b. These psalms are filled with descriptions of the ways God can shine light into your current circumstance. Take one of those descriptions and write it out below.

c. Take the passage you chose and, in your own words, re-write the psalmist's description of God.

WHAT'S IT TO YOU?

6 How would you describe or define darkness in our world today?

> **7** How does the light of the Lord provide you with hope or give you comfort when the brokenness or darkness of life seems overwhelming? Use Scripture to support your answer.

Years later, the apostle Paul wrote to encourage the church in Colossians. He prayed that they would be "strengthened with all power, according to His glorious might, for all endurance and patience with joy, giving thanks to the Father, who has qualified you to share in the inheritance of the saints in light. He has delivered us from the domain of darkness and transferred us to the kingdom of His beloved Son, in whom we have redemption, the forgiveness of sins" (Col. 1:11-14).

8 Remembering John's and Paul's assurances, take some time to journal. Focus on how Jesus's identity as the Light of the world, the light which can never be overcome, forms your identity.

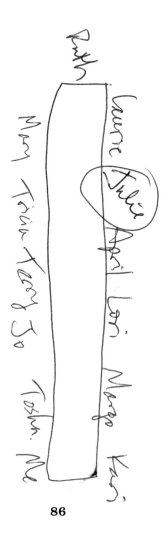

The Light of the World:
OUR VISION

"I am the light of the world. Whoever follows Me will not walk in darkness, but will have the light of life."

JOHN 8:12

THINK ABOUT IT

One of the great comforts of Scripture is found in the truth that God is not afraid of darkness. His character is not altered by brokenness, nor can the most evil of actions diminish His power. Praise be to God!

Last week you looked at both Old and New Testament passages describing the light of the Lord. Read 1 John 1:5 and reflect on one or two of the ways that the Lord has brought light into your life.

He wants me to hear His message + wants me to tell others — God is light

WHAT DO YOU SEE?

Through His teaching in John 8:12 and 9:5, Jesus declared Himself to be the Light of the world.

Read and mark the following passages from John that also use light as a descriptor for Jesus.

- With a bright color, highlight every time the word "light" is used.

- In the margin, list what John says the light is.

- In the margin, list what John says the light does.

- For every time "the light" is used, replace it with the name of Jesus.

- Then write out what Jesus is and what He does.

John 1:4-7

⁴In Him was life, and the life was the light of men. ⁵The light shines in the darkness, and the darkness has not overcome it.

⁶There was a man sent from God, whose name was John. ⁷He came as a witness, to bear

Jesus

light of men

shines —

witness about the light, that all
might believe through him.

John 3:18-21

[18]Whoever believes in Him is
not condemned, but whoever
does not believe is condemned
already, because he has not
believed in the name of the
only Son of God. [19]And this is
the judgment: the light has
come into the world, and people
loved the darkness rather than
the light because their works
were evil. [20]For everyone who
does wicked things hates the
light and does not come to the
light, lest his works should be
exposed. [21]But whoever does
what is true comes to the light,
so that it may be clearly seen
that his works have been carried
out in God."

John 12:44-46

[44]And Jesus cried out and
said, "Whoever believes in Me,
believes not in Me but in Him
who sent Me. [45]And whoever

sees Me sees Him who sent Me.
⁴⁶I have come into the world as
light, so that whoever believes
in Me may not remain in
darkness."

[handwritten: Jesus comes + saves]

From Blindness to Sight

Read John 8:58-9:41.

In chapters 7 and 8, Jesus is teaching the Pharisees and a crowd in the Temple. Chapter 8 ends with their response, an attempted stoning of Jesus for identifying Himself as the Son of God. As chapter 9 begins, Jesus had left the Temple. After removing Himself from the crowd, He performed a sign by healing a blind man in the streets of Jerusalem.

1 Why did Jesus spend all that time teaching the Pharisees about His divine identity but then choose to heal this man without their presence? (Look back at John 6:36 or forward to John 12:37 for additional help.)

[handwritten: Haven't believed even though you've seen Me. Haven't believed the miraculous signs.]

91

2 In the following charts, list some of the differences you observe between the blind man and the Pharisees in John 9.

The Blind Man

Response
to Jesus

Acceptance + belief

Jesus's
response
to him

Do you believe?

The Pharisees

Response
to Jesus

arrogance

Jesus's
response
to them

You are guilty

3 John 9:22 presents an important note on the cultural context surrounding this story.

a. The _Jewish leaders_ whom the parents feared were the leaders of the community who had religious and cultural power.

b. The _parents_ were in a vulnerable position. If they answered incorrectly, they might have been _expelled_. Being removed would have made them true outcasts, excommunicated from their extended family and all of community life.

c. After their interrogation ended in John 9:34, the Pharisees _threw out_ the man born blind. But Jesus went and _found_ him.

4 Why did the Pharisees call back the man who had been blind to their court for a second time (9:24-34) if they had already heard his testimony? What were they wanting this man to say?

What happened doesn't work with what we know.

93

WHAT DO YOU THINK?
The Healing Teacher

5 Read 1 Corinthians 11:31-32.

a. What is the difference between the way we judge ourselves and the way the Lord judges us?

Being disciplined to not be condemned.

b. This passage teaches that it is better for the Lord to judge us. Why is the Lord's judgment better than our own?

Don't want to be condemned along w/ the world.

c. John 9:39-41 reveals that yet again the Pharisees were upset with Jesus. Similar to Paul's teaching in 1 Corinthians, Jesus's teaching shows it takes humility to admit that the Lord's ways are better than our own. Take a few moments to ponder where in your own life you act as if your ways are better than the Lord's. Make a list of those areas, and use it as a guide this week, praying the Lord will shine light into those dark places.

Healing
Direction.

6 By the end of John 9, the blind man had sight. What two forms of healing did Jesus give to the man? (9:7 and 9:38)

Sight
Belief.

WHAT'S IT TO YOU?

7 Like the blind man, when Jesus is the light of a person's life, everything changes. Read the following passages and list some of the ways that living in the light of the Lord changes (or could change) your life.

ROMANS 13:11-14

Urgent - Remove dark deeds, put on right living - live decent lives. Clothe yourself w/ Jesus,

EPHESIANS 5:1-21

Live a life filled w/ love, Be thankful. Live as people of light.

1 PETER 2:9-10

We are His possession, Show others God's goodness

8 Peter and Paul acknowledged that while walking in the light is wise and good, it is not always easy.

a. What are some of the things which make "walking as children of light" (Eph. 5:8) difficult? (Try to provide specific examples from your own life.)

Used to be full of darkness

b. What are some encouragements you find from Paul's and Peter's words in Romans 13, Ephesians 5, and 1 Peter 1?

Ps 37:6

At times we choose to walk in darkness because we fail to believe the Lord has our best interest in mind. At other times we fear exposure. We have worked hard to keep certain shameful things secret, and even the thought of bringing those to light provokes anxiety. We forget the God who calls us into the light is the same God who promises to go before us, providing for and protecting us.

In closing this lesson, take time to remind yourself of the messianic promise. Read and mark Isaiah 42:1-9.

- In one color, highlight the different names for the coming Messiah.

- In another color, highlight what the Messiah will do.

- In the margins, note how you've seen Jesus fulfill these names or actions in Scripture, in history, in the lives of others, and, most importantly, in your life.

Isaiah 42:1-9

*¹Behold My servant, whom I
uphold,
My chosen, in whom My soul
delights;
I have put My Spirit upon Him;
He will bring forth justice to the
nations.
²He will not cry aloud or lift up
His voice,
or make it heard in the street;
³a bruised reed He will not
break,
and a faintly burning wick He
will not quench;
He will faithfully bring forth
justice.*

[4]He will not grow faint or be
discouraged
till He has established justice in
the earth;
and the coastlands wait for His
law.

[5]Thus says God, the LORD,
who created the heavens and
stretched them out,
who spread out the earth and
what comes from it,
who gives breath to the people
on it
and spirit to those who walk in
it:
[6]"I am the LORD; I have called
You in righteousness;
I will take You by the hand and
keep You;
I will give You as a covenant for
the people,
a light for the nations,
[7]to open the eyes that are blind,
to bring out the prisoners from
the dungeon,
from the prison those who sit in
darkness.
[8]I am the LORD; that is My

name;
My glory I give to no other,
nor my praise to carved idols.
⁹*Behold, the former things have*
come to pass,
and new things I now declare;
before they spring forth
I tell you of them."

9 In the passages from question 7, Paul and Peter declared that Christ, the Light, is able to make real change in our lives. Isaiah 42 reveals God's promise to take His people by the hand, keeping them forever in His care and protection. Take some time now to sit in prayer with the Lord. Thank God for His provision of light and salvation to His children. Ask Him to help you live in the light that He has provided through His Son Jesus.

The Door and the Good Shepherd:
GOD'S TRUSTWORTHY PROTECTION

"I am the door. If anyone enters by Me, he will be saved and will go in and out and find pasture. . . . I am the good shepherd. The good shepherd lays down His life for the sheep."

JOHN 10:9, 11

THINK ABOUT IT

Before beginning this week's lesson, take time to read through John 10:1-21.

At the end of this passage there are different responses to Jesus's words. Think of a time you have struggled to believe Jesus's teaching. What were (or are) some of the reasons you struggle with disbelief?

WHAT DO YOU SEE?

Throughout history God has been calling leaders to care for His children, but a look through Scripture reveals even the best of leaders are flawed, imperfect, and in need of God's redemption. So, just as Jesus is the truest fulfillment of the manna (bread), nourishing God's people for all time, and is the eternal light overcoming darkness forever, Jesus is also the long-awaited leader of God's people, both their faithful shepherd and ultimately the required sacrificial lamb.

False Shepherds

The role of a leader in the workplace, the home, or on a team is to help others flourish. Within the Christian faith, leaders are called specifically to help others flourish in faithful relationship with God, His Church, and the wider world.

Read and mark the passages provided as instructed.

- With a bright color, highlight every time a leadership role is mentioned.
- In a different color, mark the ways false shepherds mislead.

- In the margin, list some characteristics of false shepherds.

- If any other Bible passages on poor leadership or false shepherds come to mind, make note of them in the margins.

Jeremiah 6:13-15

*[13]"For from the least to the
greatest of them, everyone is
greedy for unjust gain;
and from prophet to priest,
everyone deals falsely.
[14]They have healed the wound of
My people lightly,
saying, 'Peace, peace,' when
there is no peace.
[15]Were they ashamed when they
committed abomination?
No, they were not at all
ashamed;
they did not know how to blush.
Therefore they shall fall among
those who fall;
at the time that I punish them,
they shall be overthrown,"
says the LORD.*

Jeremiah 50:6-7

[6]"My people have been lost

sheep. Their shepherds have led them astray, turning them away on the mountains. From mountain to hill they have gone. They have forgotten their fold. [7]All who found them have devoured them, and their enemies have said, 'We are not guilty, for they have sinned against the LORD, their habitation of righteousness, the LORD, the hope of their fathers.'"

Zephaniah 3:1-3

[1]Woe to her who is rebellious and defiled,
the oppressing city!
[2]She listens to no voice;
she accepts no correction.
She does not trust in the LORD;
she does not draw near to her God.
[3]Her officials within her
are roaring lions;
her judges are evening wolves
that leave nothing till the morning.

Matthew 7:15-20

[15]*"Beware of false prophets, who come to you in sheep's clothing but inwardly are ravenous wolves.* [16]*You will recognize them by their fruits. Are grapes gathered from thorn bushes, or figs from thistles?* [17]*So, every healthy tree bears good fruit, but the diseased tree bears bad fruit.* [18]*A healthy tree cannot bear bad fruit, nor can a diseased tree bear good fruit.* [19]*Every tree that does not bear good fruit is cut down and thrown into the fire.* [20]*Thus you will recognize them by their fruits.*

1 In your own words, what are some of the ways false shepherds mislead the Lord's people in the verses you just read and marked? What are some modern-day examples of such leadership?

The True Shepherd

God does not simply leave His people to fumble around, forever led astray by false shepherds. All of God's story is pointing towards the redemption and restoration of all things.

Read and mark the selected Old Testament passages, each promising a faithful and true Shepherd-King.

- With a bright color, highlight every time a leadership role is mentioned.

- In a different color, mark the ways the True Shepherd leads.

- In the margin, list some characteristics of the True Shepherd.

- If any other Bible passages come to mind, make note of them in the margins.

Psalm 28:8-9

*8The LORD is the strength of
His people;
He is the saving refuge of His
anointed.
9Oh, save Your people and bless
Your heritage!
Be their shepherd and carry
them forever.*

Jeremiah 23:1-6

[1]*"Woe to the shepherds who destroy and scatter the sheep of My pasture!" declares the LORD.* [2]*Therefore thus says the LORD, the God of Israel, concerning the shepherds who care for My people: "You have scattered My flock and have driven them away, and you have not attended to them. Behold, I will attend to you for your evil deeds," declares the LORD."* [3]*Then I will gather the remnant of My flock out of all the countries where I have driven them, and I will bring them back to their fold, and they shall be fruitful and multiply.* [4]*I will set shepherds over them who will care for them, and they shall fear no more, nor be dismayed, neither shall any be missing," declares the LORD.*

[5]*"Behold, the days are coming," declares the LORD, "when I will raise up for David a righteous Branch, and He shall*

reign as king and deal wisely,
and shall execute justice and
righteousness in the land. ⁶In
His days Judah will be saved,
and Israel will dwell securely.
And this is the name by which
He will be called: 'The LORD is
our righteousness.'"

Zephaniah 3:14-20

¹⁴Sing aloud, O daughter of
Zion;
shout, O Israel!
Rejoice and exult with all your
heart,
O daughter of Jerusalem!
¹⁵The LORD has taken away the
judgments against you;
He has cleared away your
enemies.
The King of Israel, the LORD, is
in your midst;
you shall never again fear evil.
¹⁶On that day it shall be said to
Jerusalem:
"Fear not, O Zion;
let not your hands grow weak.
¹⁷"The LORD your God is in
your midst,

a mighty one who will save;
He will rejoice over you with
gladness;
He will quiet you by His love;
He will exult over you with loud
singing.
[18]I will gather those of you who
mourn for the festival,
so that you will no longer suffer
reproach.
[19]Behold, at that time I will deal
with all your oppressors.
And I will save the lame
and gather the outcast,
and I will change their shame
into praise
and renown in all the earth.
[20]At that time I will bring you in,
at the time when I gather you
together;
for I will make you renowned
and praised
among all the peoples of the
earth,
when I restore your fortunes
before your eyes," says the
LORD.

Zechariah 9:16-17

[16]*On that day the LORD their
God will save them,
as the flock of His people;
for like the jewels of a crown
they shall shine on His land.*
[17]*For how great is His goodness,
and how great His beauty!
Grain shall make the young men
flourish,
and new wine the young
women.*

WHAT DO YOU THINK?

2 The passages just read and marked paint a beautiful picture of the Lord's promised safety, justice, and goodness. The Good Shepherd does not just guide and protect, but in Him alone restoration is given for the lost, justice for the oppressed, and joy for the sorrow-filled. What are some areas in your life where you feel lost, oppressed, or grieved and in need of the strong yet gentle arm of the Good Shepherd?

3 Members of the Lord's flock are able to reflect the goodness of their Shepherd in all areas of life. Based on the Old Testament verses provided above, give some examples of good shepherd-leadership in our current culture.

The Good Shepherd Brings Peace

Read Ezekiel 34:1-16; 22-31.

4 What does Ezekiel 34:10-16 say is the role of a good shepherd?

5 List three corrupt actions done by the false shepherds in Ezekiel 34:7-10.

6 What are the promises given by the Lord to His people in Ezekiel 34:22-31?

7 Using the chart provided, what are some of the similarities you notice between Ezekiel's prophecy and Jesus's teaching in John?

False Shepherds

EZEKIEL
34:1-16;
22-31

JOHN
10:1-21

The True Shepherd

EZEKIEL
34:1-16;
22-31

JOHN
10:1-21

WHAT'S IT TO YOU?

8 Think of a time you have experienced being in a leadership role (parent, small group facilitator, work, friend, or mentor).

a. Where are some areas your leadership has looked like the false shepherds?

b. Each of us has experienced anxieties, fears, and failures as leaders. Where do you see them most often creep into your leadership? What practices do you have, or can you develop, to help you identify and redirect these situations?

c. Look back over the descriptions of a good shepherd-leader. If the main goal of Christ-centered leadership is to guide others towards flourishing through love of God and His Word, how might you apply some of these characteristics to a leadership role you have now?

David the Broken yet Beautiful King

Read Psalm 23.

During his life and reign, King David knew anxiety, failure, and death. The Scriptures, many of them written by David himself, recount some of his leadership failures. Yet, David amidst his anxiety and failures could still write this peace-filled poem remembering with confidence the promises of the Lord.

9 In this well-known psalm, how did David identify the Lord?

117

10 What are some of the actions of the shepherd in this psalm? How was David comforted by the Lord's assurances in this poem?

11 The Psalms are a collection of poetry which can help the people of God navigate their emotional experiences as they worship the Lord. How might Psalm 23 help you navigate any anxiety, fear, or disappointment you are currently experiencing in your life?

12 As the true and faithful shepherd, the Lord deserves our adoration, but as a strong and mighty shepherd, He also welcomes us with open arms when we are angry or wounded. Take some time to sit with the Lord. Reread Psalm 23 and let the words of comfort be a balm for your wounds, an expression of your pain, or a way to thank the Lord for His faithful protection, provision, or care in your life.

The Door and the Good Shepherd:
OUR SECURITY AND PEACE

"I am the door. If anyone enters by Me, he will be saved and will go in and out and find pasture. . . . I am the good shepherd. The good shepherd lays down His life for the sheep."

JOHN 10:9, 11

THINK ABOUT IT

Reread either Psalm 23 or Ezekiel 34:25-31. Let the Lord's promises of restored relationship, peace, and safety speak to your heart. List how you find comfort in being one of the Lord's beloved sheep.

WHAT DO YOU SEE?
The Good Shepherd

Read and mark John 10:1-21:

- Giving each its own color, highlight any repeated words or passages.

- Circle the two identities Jesus gave Himself.

- Mark Jesus's references to others who come to the sheep.

John 10:1-21

1"Truly, truly, I say to you, he who does not enter the sheepfold by the door but climbs in by another way, that man is a thief and a robber. 2But he who enters by the door is the shepherd of the sheep. 3To him the gatekeeper opens. The sheep hear his voice, and he calls his own sheep by name and leads them out. 4When he has brought out all his own, he goes before them, and the sheep follow him, for they know his voice. *⁵A stranger they will not follow, but they will flee from him, for they do not know the voice of strangers." ⁶This figure of speech Jesus used with them, but they did not understand what He was saying to them.*

⁷So Jesus again said to them, "Truly, truly, I say to you, I am the door of the sheep. ⁸All who came before Me are thieves and robbers, but the sheep did not listen to them. ⁹I am the door. If anyone enters by Me, he will be saved and will go in and out and find pasture. ¹⁰The thief comes only to steal and kill and destroy. I came that they may have life and have it abundantly. ¹¹I am the good shepherd. The good shepherd lays down His life for the sheep. ¹²He who is a hired hand and not a shepherd, who does not own the sheep, sees the wolf coming and leaves the sheep and flees, and the wolf snatches them and scatters them. ¹³He flees because he is a hired hand and cares nothing for the sheep. ¹⁴I am the good shepherd. I know My own and My own know Me, ¹⁵just as the Father knows Me and I know the Father; and I lay down My life for the sheep. ¹⁶And I have other sheep that are not of this fold. I must bring them also, and they will listen to My voice. So there will be one flock, one shepherd. ¹⁷For this reason the Father loves Me, because I lay down My life that I may take it up again. ¹⁸No one takes it from Me, but I lay it down of My own accord. I have authority to lay it down, and I have authority to take it up again. This charge I have received from My Father."

¹⁹There was again a division among the Jews because of these words. ²⁰Many of them said, "He has a demon, and is insane; why listen to Him?" ²¹Others said, "These are not the words of one who is oppressed by a demon. Can a demon open the eyes of the blind?"

1 What contrast did Jesus make between His actions as the Good Shepherd and that of the thief or the hired hand?

2 What is the unique role of the Good Shepherd?

3 Quickly reviewing John 9 and 10 (see the passages that follow), how did Jesus act as a protective door and shepherd for each of the following?

The Blind Man

JOHN
9:6-7,
35-39

Jesus's Followers

JOHN
9:1-3;
10:1-21

The Pharisees

JOHN
9:40-41;
10:1-21

WHAT DO YOU THINK?

The Bible aptly uses sheep as an illustration of the unfaithfulness of mankind towards the Lord. Like sheep, we are constantly wandering off, getting stuck in the mud and deep pits of our sin. We need rescuing and guidance. Yet, as we read in John 9, the Pharisees were enraged by both Jesus's proclamation of His identity and by His audacity to name that they, too, needed Him for atonement. Instead of acting in humility towards Jesus's teaching, the Pharisees responded in arrogance and violence and, ultimately, by crucifying Jesus, the Good Shepherd and Sacrificial Lamb.

When we go astray, we have the option, like the Pharisees and the disciples, to respond to the pursuit of the Good Shepherd. Take a few moments to reflect on how you typically respond when your need for Jesus's mercy is exposed.

The Shepherd and the Lamb

Read Isaiah 52:13–53:12.

4 What is Isaiah's description of the people in 53:6?

5 List the adjectives used to describe the Servant in 53:7.

6 What does Isaiah say, in 53:11-12, will be accomplished by the sacrifice of the Lamb?

7 Look at John 1:29. How does John the Baptist identify Jesus? (Fill in the blank below.)

"The next day he saw Jesus coming toward him, and said, "_____

_____!"

WHAT'S IT TO YOU?

8 Through the power of the Holy Spirit, the Good Shepherd is still actively pursuing and redirecting His flock. Besides the Bible, what other tools do we have to help us learn and apply the wisdom of the Good Shepherd in our lives?

9 Take a moment to reflect on your own life.

a. What are some of the false voices which currently speak into your life?

b. What are their messages to you?

c. In what ways do their messages attempt to "steal and kill and destroy" the abundant life offered to you by the Good Shepherd?

d. Read John 10:27-30. How might Jesus's words help comfort and support you as you interact with the messages attempting to cause destruction in your life?

Read and mark Revelation 5.

* Highlight the phrases that show who the Lamb is.

* Mark the reason the Lamb can open the scroll.

* In the margins name who is identified as the Lamb in this scene.

* In a new color, highlight the new song of the congregation

* In yet another color, highlight the Lamb's reward in verse 12.

Revelation 5

¹Then I saw in the right hand of Him who was seated on the throne a scroll written within and on the back, sealed with seven seals. ²And I saw a mighty angel proclaiming with a loud voice, "Who is worthy to open the scroll and break its seals?"

³And no one in heaven or on
earth or under the earth was
able to open the scroll or to
look into it, ⁴and I began to
weep loudly because no one was
found worthy to open the scroll
or to look into it. ⁵And one of
the elders said to me, "Weep
no more; behold, the Lion of
the tribe of Judah, the Root of
David, has conquered, so that
He can open the scroll and its
seven seals."

⁶And between the throne and
the four living creatures and
among the elders I saw a Lamb
standing, as though it had been
slain, with seven horns and with
seven eyes, which are the seven
spirits of God sent out into all
the earth. ⁷And He went and
took the scroll from the right
hand of Him who was seated
on the throne. ⁸And when He
had taken the scroll, the four
living creatures and the twenty-
four elders fell down before the
Lamb, each holding a harp, and

*golden bowls full of incense,
which are the prayers of the
saints. [9]And they sang a new
song, saying,*

*"Worthy are You to take the
scroll and to open its seals,
for You were slain, and by Your
blood You ransomed people for
God
from every tribe and language
and people and nation,
[10]and You have made them a
kingdom and priests to our God,
and they shall reign on the
earth."
[11]Then I looked, and I heard
around the throne and the
living creatures and the elders
the voice of many angels,
numbering myriads of myriads
and thousands of thousands,
[12]saying with a loud voice,
"Worthy is the Lamb who was
slain,
to receive power and wealth and
wisdom and might
and honor and glory and
blessing!"*

^{13}*And I heard every creature in*
heaven and on earth and under
the earth and in the sea, and all
that is in them, saying,
"To Him who sits on the throne
and to the Lamb
be blessing and honor and glory
and might forever and ever!"
^{14}*And the four living creatures*
said, "Amen!" and the elders fell
down and worshiped.

10 In John 10:11-18, Jesus identified Himself as the Good Shepherd. With the Isaiah and Revelation passages in mind, explain how Jesus can be both the Shepherd and the Lamb?

11 Jesus is the Door, protecting His people from those who would do them eternal harm. He is the True and Good Shepherd, providing guidance and security for His sheep. And He is the sacrificial Lamb, come to "take away the sins of the world!" (John 1:29). As one of His sheep, with John 10 and Revelation 5 in mind, how can His identity as Protector and Provider help you understand your own identity?

12 To close this week's lesson, read Hebrews 10:11-18 and note the promises of restoration made by the Lord to His sheep. Take some time to journal a prayer of confession, or of thanksgiving, or a cry for deliverance.

The Resurrection and the Life:
GOD'S PLAN OF RESTORATION

"Jesus said to her, 'I am the resurrection and the life. Whoever believes in Me, though he die, yet shall he live.'"

JOHN 11:25

THINK ABOUT IT

Along with the "I Am" statements, the book of John records many of Jesus's miraculous signs. John 20:30-31 states:

> *Now Jesus did many other signs in the presence of the disciples, which are not written in this book; but these are written so that you may believe that Jesus is the Christ, the Son of God, and that by believing you may have life in His name.*

List some of the miraculous signs Jesus performed during His earthly ministry. Take a moment to think about why Jesus performed these signs. What are some of the things they can teach us about Jesus?

The Past Fulfilled, the Future Foretold

With the first four "I Am" statements, Jesus was calling His audience to remember the stories and prophecies woven throughout the Old Testament books, reminding them the Lord's promised faithfulness does not change.

Identifying as the Bread of Life, Jesus taught that He is the true eternal fulfillment of the Lord's provision. As the Light of the world, Jesus showed He is the long-awaited pure light which overcomes the darkness of this world. As the Door, Jesus explained He is the one who identifies and admits the sheep into His Father's flock. And as the Good Shepherd, Jesus identified Himself as the protector of the Lord's family.

With the last three "I Am" statements, we come to the climax of Jesus's earthly ministry. Jesus began His journey back to Jerusalem, the long walk which He knew would end with His painful crucifixion. His identity statements, which previously had been given in public for anyone to hear, were now given in private moments with only His closest followers. With the end of His earthly mission at hand, Jesus revealed that He was not just the fulfillment of Old Testament prophecy, but He had come to usher in a new dawn. Christ fulfilled the old covenants and established a new covenant, a promise of eternal life amidst a dying world.

WHAT DO YOU SEE?

Take some time to read John 11:1-44 in its entirety.

1 Before unpacking John 11, take a moment to look closely at the story of Lazarus. Use the space below to write out any observations (repetition, contrasts, actions, or statements that stand out to you), and any questions you have while reading the story.

Observations

Questions

The Patient and Loving Lord

2 From the beginning of this account Jesus was honest about His intentions. What did Jesus tell the disciples was going to happen? Why did Jesus say He was speaking so plainly with His disciples? (See John 11:4 and 13-15.)

3 What do verses 11:3 and 11:5 tell us about the relationship between Lazarus, his sisters, and Jesus?

4 What was Jesus's response in 11:4 and 6 when He received word that Lazarus was sick?

WHAT DO YOU THINK?
Lazarus's Sisters

For a review of the relationship between Mary, Martha, and Jesus, you can read their first encounter with Jesus, found in Luke 10:38-42.

5 Have you ever pondered Jesus's actions before His return to Bethany? Take a moment to let yourself think about the tension felt by those involved in this story. Make a list of thoughts or emotions Mary and Martha may have felt towards Jesus as their brother fell ill, suffered, and then died.

Jesus and Martha

Read and mark John 11:17-27.

- Highlight Martha's response when she saw Jesus arriving.

- Mark any elements of doubt or misunderstanding in Martha's interaction with Jesus.

- In another color mark any elements of faith in Martha's interaction with Jesus.

John 11:17-27

¹⁷*Now when Jesus came, He found that Lazarus had already been in the tomb four days. ¹⁸Bethany was near Jerusalem, about two miles off, ¹⁹and many of the Jews had come to Martha and Mary to console them concerning their brother. ²⁰So when Martha heard that Jesus was coming, she went and met Him, but Mary remained seated in the house. ²¹Martha said to Jesus, "Lord, if You had been here, my brother would not have died. ²²But even now I know that whatever You ask from God, God will give You." ²³Jesus said to her, "Your brother will rise again." ²⁴Martha said to Him, "I know that he will rise again in the resurrection on the last day." ²⁵Jesus said to her, "I am the resurrection and the life. Whoever believes in Me, though he die, yet shall he live, ²⁶and*

*everyone who lives and believes
in Me shall never die. Do you
believe this?"* [27]*She said to Him,
"Yes, Lord; I believe that You are
the Christ, the Son of God, who
is coming into the world."*

6 From their conversation, what can be observed about how Jesus met Martha in her grief?

7 During their conversation Jesus declared Himself as the Resurrection and the Life. How does the conversation in 11:21-27 show Martha's understanding of Jesus's identity? In what ways does it also reveal her incomplete understanding of Jesus?

Jesus and Mary

Read and mark John 11:28-36.

- Highlight Mary's response when she saw Jesus arriving.

- Mark any elements of doubt in Mary's interaction with Jesus.

- In another color mark any elements of faith in Mary's interaction with Jesus.

John 11:28-36

28When she had said this, she went and called her sister Mary, saying in private, "The Teacher is here and is calling for you." 29And when she heard it, she rose quickly and went to Him. 30Now Jesus had not yet come into the village but was still in the place where Martha had met Him. 31When the Jews who were with her in the house, consoling her, saw Mary rise quickly and go out, they followed her, supposing that she was going to the tomb to weep there. 32Now when Mary came to where Jesus was and saw Him, she fell at His feet, saying to Him, "Lord, if

You had been here, my brother would not have died." ³³When Jesus saw her weeping, and the Jews who had come with her also weeping, He was deeply moved in His spirit and greatly troubled. ³⁴And He said, "Where have you laid him?" They said to him, "Lord, come and see." ³⁵Jesus wept. ³⁶So the Jews said, "See how He loved him!"

8 How does their conversation reveal Jesus's comfort of Mary in her grief?

9 Look back at the Martha and Mary passages.

a. In the margins make note of the differences you notice in the way the two sisters grieved the death of their brother in these passages.

b. How did Jesus meet each sister with compassion amid her differing expression of grief?

c. In what ways could the different encounters between Jesus and the sisters bring comfort to us or to those around us in the midst of grief or pain?

WHAT'S IT TO YOU?

As a teenager, Joni Eareckson Tada was paralyzed in a diving accident, leaving her wheelchair-dependent. For the last 50 years, Mrs. Tada has spent a good portion of her life sharing the lessons, both the joy-filled and the sorrow-filled, she has learned through her suffering. In one of her most famous quotes she teaches, at times "God permits what He hates to accomplish what He loves."[4] Her statement can be used as a tool to help understand John 11. Jesus chose not to return to Bethany the moment He heard of Lazarus's illness. Jesus loved Lazarus and his sisters, and yet He allowed Lazarus's illness and death to occur.

10 In the next chapter of this study, we will look more closely at Jesus's resurrection of Lazarus. But before moving on to the resolution, it is necessary to wrestle with the complexities found in John 11:14-15. Jesus loved Lazarus and his sisters, and yet, when they were in despair, He waited. Jesus knew Lazarus's illness would lead to death, and yet He waited.

a. What do you think Mrs. Tada's quote means and how might it help explain what Jesus is teaching His followers (then and now) in these passages?

b. Think of a time in your past when you have waited for something. How did you respond to the Lord during that season of waiting or distress? In what ways did that season change your relationship with the Lord?

c. How might the Lord be using a season of distress or waiting in your life currently?

Until the Lord returns, everyone is in some season of waiting. Whether we're waiting for an illness's diagnosis or treatment, for a spouse, for job clarification, or for a relationship's healing, life is filled with a variety of griefs and distress, but ultimately every member of God's family is waiting for the day we will get to fall into the waiting arms of our Heavenly Father.

11 In closing, take encouragement from the restoring promises of God. Read through the closing lines of Zephaniah, taking time to cry out in prayer to the Lord. Ask the Lord to help carry the fear, grief, or distress you feel in this season of waiting. Remember, Jesus loved Mary, Martha, Lazarus, and His followers, and yet He waited. He waited because, despite their current pain, He knew the long-term plan of God was for their good. He waited because He knew that His Father is trustworthy. He waited because He knew every promise His Father has made will be fulfilled.

Zephaniah 3:14-20

[14]*Sing aloud, O daughter of Zion;*
shout, O Israel!
Rejoice and exult with all your heart,
O daughter of Jerusalem!
[15]*The LORD has taken away the judgments against you;*
he has cleared away your enemies.
The King of Israel, the LORD, is

in your midst;
you shall never again fear evil.
¹⁶On that day it shall be said to
Jerusalem:
"Fear not, O Zion;
let not your hands grow weak.
¹⁷"The LORD your God is in
your midst,
a mighty one who will save;
He will rejoice over you with
gladness;
He will quiet you by His love;
He will exult over you with loud
singing.
¹⁸I will gather those of you who
mourn for the festival,
so that you will no longer suffer
reproach.
¹⁹Behold, at that time I will deal
with all your oppressors.
And I will save the lame
and gather the outcast,
and I will change their shame
into praise
and renown in all the earth.
²⁰At that time I will bring you in,
at the time when I gather you
together;
for I will make you renowned

and praised
among all the peoples of the
earth,
when I restore your fortunes
before your eyes," says the
LORD.

The Resurrection and the Life:
OUR DIVINE PHYSICIAN

"Jesus said to her, 'I am the resurrection and the life. Whoever believes in Me, though he die, yet shall he live.'"

JOHN 11:25

THINK ABOUT IT

Read John 11:1-44

First Impressions: Jesus is constantly doing the unexpected, taking what people think they know and pointing them to a greater understanding of God, the Law, or His identity. Each time He does the unexpected, it causes change (realization of brokenness, new faith, or increased love of God).

List some of the ways Jesus did the unexpected in John 11:1-44. Then think of a time when the Lord expanded your understanding of the Law or His identity. How did that experience shape you to be who you are today?

WHAT DO YOU SEE?
Grief and Glory

Jesus was always intentional with His words and actions. To gain insight into some of Jesus's intentions, use the instructions below to observe and analyze the passage provided.

- Underline Jesus's "I am" statement.

- Highlight Jesus's responses to the grief of Lazarus's friends and family.

- Based on the things you know or have learned about Jesus, use the margins to list some of the reasons Jesus was troubled, moved, and wept.

John 11:24-44

[24]Martha said to Him, "I know that he will rise again in the resurrection on the last day." [25]Jesus said to her, "I am the resurrection and the life. Whoever believes in Me, though he die, yet shall he live, [26]and everyone who lives and believes in Me shall never die. Do you believe this?" [27]She said to Him, "Yes, Lord; I believe that You are

the Christ, the Son of God, who
is coming into the world."

28When she had said this, she
went and called her sister Mary,
saying in private, "The Teacher
is here and is calling for you."
29And when she heard it, she
rose quickly and went to Him.
30Now Jesus had not yet come
into the village but was still in
the place where Martha had met
Him. 31When the Jews who were
with her in the house, consoling
her, saw Mary rise quickly
and go out, they followed her,
supposing that she was going to
the tomb to weep there. 32Now
when Mary came to where Jesus
was and saw Him, she fell at His
feet, saying to Him, "Lord, if
You had been here, my brother
would not have died." 33When
Jesus saw her weeping, and the
Jews who had come with her
also weeping, He was deeply
moved in His spirit and greatly
troubled. 34And He said, "Where
have you laid him?" They said

to Him, "Lord, come and see."
[35]Jesus wept. [36]So the Jews said,
"See how He loved him!" [37]But
some of them said, "Could not
He who opened the eyes of the
blind man also have kept this
man from dying?"

[38]Then Jesus, deeply moved
again, came to the tomb. It was
a cave, and a stone lay against
it. [39]Jesus said, "Take away the
stone." Martha, the sister of the
dead man, said to Him, "Lord,
by this time there will be an
odor, for he has been dead four
days." [40]Jesus said to her, "Did I
not tell you that if you believed
you would see the glory of
God?" [41]So they took away the
stone. And Jesus lifted up His
eyes and said, "Father, I thank
You that You have heard Me.
[42]I knew that You always hear
Me, but I said this on account
of the people standing around,
that they may believe that You
sent Me." [43]When He had said
these things, He cried out with a

loud voice, "Lazarus, come out."
*⁴⁴The man who had died came
out, his hands and feet bound
with linen strips, and his face
wrapped with a cloth. Jesus said
to them, "Unbind him, and let
him go."*

1 What did Jesus do just before He raised Lazarus from the dead?

2 What statement of confidence did Jesus make in John 11:41-42?

3 Read Genesis 1:3 and 1:26. What did God do in these passages to create?

4 What did Jesus do in John 11:43 to cause Lazarus to come back to life?

WHAT DO YOU THINK?

5 If Jesus knew He was going to raise Lazarus from the dead, why do you think He prayed to the Father? What does this show about His relationship with the Father?

6 What do Genesis 1 and John 11:43 reveal about the power of the Lord?

7 The Book of Revelation, also written by John, is a description of God's ultimate restoration of His people. Read Revelation 21:1-4, then use the following questions to help you understand how Jesus's words and actions in John 11 relate to God's larger story.

Revelation 21:1-4

¹*Then I saw a new heaven and a new earth, for the first heaven and the first earth had passed away, and the sea was no more. ²And I saw the holy city, new Jerusalem, coming down out of heaven from God, prepared as a bride adorned for her husband. ³And I heard a loud voice from the throne saying, "Behold, the dwelling place of God is with man. He will dwell with them, and they will be His people, and God Himself will be with them as their God. ⁴He will wipe away every tear from their eyes, and death shall be no more, neither shall there be mourning, nor crying, nor pain anymore, for*

*the former things have passed
away."*

a. Look back through John 11 and at your responses in the last chapter. Then make a list of Jesus's different responses to Lazarus's illness and death, including His interactions with the others in the story.

b. When the Lord redeems all things, He promises to wipe away every tear from the eyes of His beloved children. Jesus knew the different personalities and emotions of each person in this story. In your own words, how can the picture in Revelation 21:1-4, of the new heavens and the new earth, help you better understand Jesus's different reactions to His friend's death?

c. Name some of the ways these words from Revelation can give you hope in the midst of sorrow.

WHAT'S IT TO YOU?

8 Look back again at John 11:25-26. Every person involved in this story eventually died, even Lazarus was one day placed back in a stone tomb a second time. With the John 11 and Revelation 21 passages in mind, explain what Jesus meant when He proclaimed, "I am the resurrection and the life. Whoever believes in Me, though he die, yet shall he live."

9 Throughout the book of John, Jesus repeatedly identified Himself as the source of eternal life. In Romans 6:3-5, Paul, conveying the union believers have with Christ, taught, "Do you not know that all of us who have been baptized into Christ Jesus were baptized into His death? We were buried therefore with Him by baptism into death, in order that, just as Christ was raised from the dead by the glory of the Father, we too might walk in newness of life. For if we have been united with Him in a death like His, we shall certainly be united with Him in a resurrection like His."

a. In your own words how do Paul's teaching and Jesus's identity statement in John 11:25 define the new identity given to those who believe in Christ?

b. Give examples of how being united with Christ's death and resurrection helps (or could help) give you more understanding of Paul's encouragement to "walk in newness of life" (Rom. 6:4).

10 Think of a time when you struggled with faith. If you could go back and coach yourself using the promises of Jesus in John 11, the teaching of Paul from Romans 6, or the vision seen by John in Revelation 5, what would you have said to yourself?

11 Take a moment to dream. What could life look like if you lived daily in the reality that "we shall certainly be united with Him in a resurrection like His" (Rom. 6:5)? Then write out or discuss practical ways this can be realized in your life.

John 11 helps give insight into some of the tension that Jesus experienced in His time on earth. The humanity of Christ married with His divinity helps show how Jesus felt grief and hope, exercised patience and anger; His tenderness and supremacy were on display throughout His earthly mission. Jesus loved His friends and let His friends endure pain. Lazarus suffered unto death, while his sisters endured the heart-wrenching devastation that comes with the death of a loved one. These passages show us that Jesus had insight into exactly what was happening, and yet He waited; His loved ones suffered, and Lazarus died. Praise God the story does not end at Lazarus's death or even at the celebration of his resurrection. Jesus came not to raise one man from the dead, but to die Himself and, in His own resurrection, give new life to all who believe in Him. The suffering of Lazarus and his sisters was redeemed in Christ, just as the suffering of all of God's children is redeemed in Christ because by His suffering, the suffering of the Sacrificial Lamb, God's children are saved. Thus, the real power of these passages lies not in Jesus's defeat of death one time in Bethany, but in His defeat of death for all time on Calvary.

12 In closing, read back through Revelation 21:1-4. Since the beginning, God's story has been about redemption and restoration. Take some time to pray and journal. Thank the Lord for the good things He has done in your story and ask the Lord to reveal His resurrection power in the midst of your suffering. Then pray He will give you a renewed hope in the beautiful promises of Revelation 21:1-4.

The Way, the Truth, and the Life:
GOD'S PROVIDED HOLY LAMB

*"Let not your hearts be troubled . . . I am
the way, and the truth, and the life. No one
comes to the Father except through Me."*

JOHN 14:1a, 6

THINK ABOUT IT

In raising Lazarus from the dead, Jesus did the unthinkable. His power and purpose on display caused many to love and believe in His divine authority, yet not everyone saw His life-giving mission as worthy of praise. Read John 12:42-43. What do you think was John's purpose in including this statement in his teaching?

In his first twelve chapters, John covered three years of Jesus's broad missional work. These chapters recount Jesus's teaching, miraculous signs, and interactions with a variety of people—from crowds of strangers and religious leaders to His dedicated followers and disciples. However, in chapters 13-17, there is a change of tone and audience as the story slows to a snail's pace. Jesus and a small group of His closest followers were back in Jerusalem in a private room, away from the large crowds and constant judgment of the religious leaders. On that Thursday evening they shared one last meal, and over the course of five chapters, Jesus gave them one last message, a final discourse.

WHAT DO YOU SEE?
Passover

John 13:1 begins with the thesis statement of Jesus's final discourse.

> *"Now before the Feast of the Passover, when Jesus knew that His hour had come to depart out of this world to the Father, having loved His own who were in the world, He loved them to the end."*

1 As He prepared to teach His followers that evening, what does John tell us that "Jesus knew"?

2 To whom was John referring when he said, "His own"? (Think back also to John 10:3, 4, 14-15.)

3 Thinking back over what you have learned so far in this study, give three examples of Jesus's signs, actions, or teachings that John recorded which reveal Christ's love for "His own."

John, in his teaching, wanted to make sure his readers, past and present, understood the role Jesus plays in the whole of God's story. One of the ways John did this was by making note of the Jewish feasts which occurred around various points in Jesus's ministry. These are not just simple points of reference, but they continue to make the connections to prove Jesus is the fulfillment of many of God's promises.

4 What feast is mentioned in John 13:1?

Read and mark the following passages from Exodus 10 and 12.

- Highlight references to specific time markers.

- Circle each person involved in this passage.

- In another color, highlight any repeated words.

- In the margins make note of any additional questions you may have after reading these passages.

Exodus 10:27-29

27But the LORD hardened Pharaoh's heart, and he would not let them go. 28Then Pharaoh said to him, "Get away from me; take care never to see my face again, for on the day you see my face you shall die." 29Moses said, "As you say! I will not see your face again."

Exodus 12:1-7, 12-14, 21

*¹The LORD said to Moses and
Aaron in the land of Egypt,
²"This month shall be for you
the beginning of months. It
shall be the first month of
the year for you. ³Tell all the
congregation of Israel that on
the tenth day of this month
every man shall take a lamb
according to their fathers'
houses, a lamb for a household.
⁴And if the household is too
small for a lamb, then he and
his nearest neighbor shall take
according to the number of
persons; according to what each
can eat you shall make your
count for the lamb. ⁵Your lamb
shall be without blemish, a male
a year old. You may take it from
the sheep or from the goats,
⁶and you shall keep it until the
fourteenth day of this month,
when the whole assembly of the
congregation of Israel shall kill
their lambs at twilight. ⁷"Then
they shall take some of the blood
and put it on the two doorposts*

and the lintel of the houses in
which they eat it.

[12]For I will pass through the
land of Egypt that night, and
I will strike all the firstborn in
the land of Egypt, both man
and beast; and on all the gods of
Egypt I will execute judgments:
I am the LORD. [13]The blood
shall be a sign for you, on the
houses where you are. And
when I see the blood, I will pass
over you, and no plague will
befall you to destroy you, when I
strike the land of Egypt. [14]"This
day shall be for you a memorial
day, and you shall keep it as a
feast to the LORD; throughout
your generations, as a statute
forever, you shall keep it as a
feast.

[21]"Then Moses called all the
elders of Israel and said to
them, "Go and select lambs for
yourselves according to your
clans, and kill the Passover
lamb."

5 Exodus 12 established the Feast of
_____.

6 What had happened in Exodus chapters 7-11 that led to God's final act against the Egyptians?

7 Why were the Jewish people instructed to cover the doorframes of their homes with the blood of a lamb? What did the mark of blood symbolize?

8 Passover served as a reminder to the Jewish people that _____ had to be shed for the protection of their life.

9 After reading through the above Exodus account, in your own words, explain why John started his retelling of Jesus's final discourse by reminding his readers that the event took place on the eve of Passover? What connection was John making for his readers? (For a hint, see John the Baptist's proclamation in John 1:29 and see Revelation 5:6-13.)

WHAT DO YOU THINK?
A Cleansing Love

Read and mark the following passages from John 13:3-17, 34-35.

- Circle the name of each person involved in this passage.

- Underline Jesus's actions.

- Highlight the words of teaching Jesus gave His disciples.

- In another color, highlight Jesus's command.

John 13:3-17, 34-35

³Jesus, knowing that the Father had given all things into His hands, and that He had come from God and was going back to God, ⁴rose from supper. He laid aside His outer garments, and taking a towel, tied it around His waist. ⁵Then He poured water into a basin and began to wash the disciples' feet and to wipe them with the towel that was wrapped around Him. ⁶He came to Simon Peter, who said to Him, "Lord, do You wash my feet?" ⁷Jesus answered him, "What I am doing you do not understand now, but afterward you will understand." ⁸Peter said to Him, "You shall never wash my feet." Jesus answered him, "If I do not wash you, you have no share with Me." ⁹Simon Peter said to Him, "Lord, not my feet only but also my hands and my head!" ¹⁰Jesus said to him, "The one who has bathed does not need to wash, except for his feet, but is completely clean. And you are clean, but not every one of you." ¹¹For He knew who was to betray Him; that was why He said, "Not all of you are clean."

¹²When He had washed their feet and put on His outer garments and resumed His place, He said to them, "Do you understand what I have done to you? ¹³You call Me Teacher and Lord, and you are right, for so I am. ¹⁴If I then, your Lord and Teacher, have washed your feet, you also ought to wash one another's feet. ¹⁵For I have given you an example, that you also should do just as I have done to you. ¹⁶Truly, truly, I say to you, a servant is not greater than his master, nor is a messenger greater than the one who sent him. ¹⁷If you know these things, blessed are you if you do them.

³⁴A new commandment I give to you, that you love one another: just as I have loved you, you also are to love one another. ³⁵By this all people will know that you are

My disciples, if you have love for one another."

10 Throughout His teaching ministry Jesus was constantly telling stories, using metaphors and parables to illustrate important lessons. In John 13, using the common practice of foot washing, Jesus enacted the lesson He was teaching. List three teaching points you see that Jesus made in the example He gave.

1.

2.

3.

11 Read Deuteronomy 6:4-6 and Leviticus 19:18. What similarities do you notice between these Old Testament commands and the command Jesus was giving His disciples in John 13:34-35?

The Son of Man

After Judas left the upper room (headed to betray Jesus to the waiting Jewish officials), Jesus began to deliver the message of His final discourse. "Son of Man" was one of Jesus's most frequently used titles for Himself (see also Matt. 9:6, Mark 10:45, Luke 9:22). And on this evening, Jesus wanted to make His divine identity exceptionally clear, so He again drew on Old Testament passages to help His disciples understand His role in the fulfillment of God's restorative plan.

Read and mark Daniel 7:13-14.

- Circle each person involved in this passage.

- Underline what was given to the Son of Man.

- Highlight any promises given in this passage.

Daniel 7:13-14

[13]*"I saw in the night visions,
and behold, with the clouds of
heaven
there came One like a Son of
Man,
and He came to the Ancient of
Days
and was presented before Him.*
[14]*And to Him was given
dominion
and glory and a kingdom,
that all peoples, nations, and
languages
should serve Him;
His dominion is an everlasting
dominion,
which shall not pass away,
and His kingdom one that shall
not be destroyed.*

12 From this passage in Daniel, what is the glory given to the Son of Man?

13 After reading Daniel, what statement do you think Jesus was making to His disciples at the beginning of His final message in John 13:31-32?

WHAT'S IT TO YOU?
The Humble Servant Leader

Jesus knew Judas's heart. He knew His friend was about to hurt Him deeply, and yet, Jesus still knelt before Judas and washed his feet. In later chapters John recounts that after Jesus was arrested, the apostles all hid, and Peter denied ever knowing Jesus. The Son of Man knew the selfish sinful hearts of every person in the room that night and still He chose love, humility, and sacrifice. His cleansing of their feet offered a simple yet profound illustration. Jesus, the Son of Man in both His humanity and in His divinity is truly "the Lamb of God, who takes away the sin of the world!"

14 Jesus washed the disciple's feet, proclaimed His divinity, and then, and only then, did He ask the disciples to act. Read John 13:34-35. What action did Jesus ask of His followers?

15 In this story, Jesus showed His love by physically washing His disciples' feet. Where in your own life is there an opportunity for you to offer loving service to someone? What hesitations do you have in serving that person? Why?

John begins and ends this section of teaching pointing out Jesus's love for His people (John 13:1, 34-35). But it is important to remember that Jesus is continuing the loving work that the Lord has been doing amongst His people for thousands of years. As one example, the Lord used the prophet Jeremiah to call His people to repentance, reminding them "I have loved you with an everlasting love; therefore I have continued my faithfulness to you" (Jer. 31:3). All of history is the story of God's loving restoration of His people.

16 The Scriptures give us all kinds of examples of people who knew God yet did not trust in His love.

a. What parts of your own story cause you to struggle to trust in the Lord's love?

b. Name some of the emotions you feel or actions you take when you fail to believe the Lord loves you.

c. Where are other places in Scripture you can look to be reminded of God's love for you?

17 In closing this lesson, take some time to sit in prayer or to journal with thanksgiving for the Lord's unfailing, faithful, everlasting love.

". . .having loved His own who were in the world, He loved them to the end."

JOHN 13:1B

"I have loved you with an everlasting love; therefore I have continued My faithfulness to you."

JEREMIAH 31:3

The Way, the Truth, and the Life:
OUR ONLY PATH

"Let not your hearts be troubled . . . I am the way, and the truth, and the life. No one comes to the Father except through Me."

JOHN 14:1a, 6

THINK ABOUT IT

On the eve of Passover, Jesus gave His disciples a farewell message. If you knew you were going to have one last conversation with someone you loved. What would you say? What advice or comfort would you want to convey?

WHAT DO YOU SEE?
God's Unfaithful People

God is clear about what He wants from His children. Writing through Moses, He proclaims, "Hear, O Israel: The LORD our God, the LORD is one. You shall love the LORD your God with all your heart and with all your soul and with all your might. And these words I command you today shall be on your heart. . . . It is the LORD your God you shall fear. . . .You shall not go after other gods" (Deut. 6:4-5, 13, 14). Even with a direct command, the people of Israel consistently turned against the Lord. They did not follow His way, believe His truth, or desire life with Him.

1 Before we go further into John 14, let's take a moment to look back. Use the chart provided to review a few of the times in history when God's people struggled to remember His way and truth.

The Unfaithful or Forgetful Actions of God's People

DEUTERONOMY
1:19-36

JUDGES
2:11;
3:7, 12; 4:1

ZEPHANIAH
3:1-7

The One Faithful Son

Read and mark the following passages from John 14.

- Underline each time Jesus asked the disciples to know or believe.

- Highlight Jesus's "I Am" statement.

- In another color highlight any command Jesus gave.

- In a third color highlight any mention of the "Helper."

- In the margin answer the question: Who is the Helper?

John 14:1-11, 15-18, 25-31

¹*"Let not your hearts be troubled. Believe in God; believe also in Me.* ²*In My Father's house are many rooms. If it were not so, would I have told you that I go to prepare a place for you?* ³*And if I go and prepare a place for you, I will come again and will take you to Myself, that where I am you may be also.* ⁴*And you know the way to where I am going."* ⁵*Thomas said to Him, "Lord, we do not know where You are going. How can we know the way?"* ⁶*Jesus said to him, "I am the way, and the truth, and the life. No one comes to the Father except through Me.* ⁷*If you had known Me, you would have known My Father also. From now on you do know Him and have seen Him."*

⁸Philip said to Him, "Lord, show us the Father, and it is enough for us." ⁹Jesus said to him, "Have I been with you so long, and you still do not know Me, Philip? Whoever has seen Me has seen the Father. How can you say, 'Show us the Father'? ¹⁰Do you not believe that I am in the Father and the Father is in Me? The words that I say to you I do not speak on My own authority, but the Father who dwells in Me does His works. ¹¹Believe Me that I am in the Father and the Father is in Me, or else believe on account of the works themselves.

¹⁵"If you love Me, you will keep My commandments. ¹⁶And I will ask the Father, and He will give you another Helper, to be with you forever, ¹⁷even the Spirit of truth, whom the world cannot receive, because it neither sees Him nor knows Him. You know Him, for He dwells with you and will be in you.

[18]"I will not leave you as orphans; I will come to you. [19]Yet a little while and the world will see Me no more, but you will see Me. Because I live, you also will live.

[25]"These things I have spoken to you while I am still with you. [26]But the Helper, the Holy Spirit, whom the Father will send in My name, He will teach you all things and bring to your remembrance all that I have said to you. [27]Peace I leave with you; My peace I give to you. Not as the world gives, do I give to you. Let not your hearts be troubled, neither let them be afraid. [28]You heard Me say to you, 'I am going away, and I will come to you.' If you loved Me, you would have rejoiced, because I am going to the Father, for the Father is greater than I. [29]And now I have told you before it takes place, so that when it does take place you may believe. [30]I will no longer talk much with you, for the

ruler of this world is coming. He has no claim on Me, ³¹but I do as the Father has commanded Me, so that the world may know that I love the Father. Rise, let us go from here.

2 Remember that John 13-17 is all one continuous lesson. Look back to John 13:33-38 and read Jesus's words from earlier in the evening. What did Jesus say to His disciples that caused them to be troubled?

3 Which disciples question Jesus in these verses? What were their questions?

4 Jesus answers all their questions in John 14:6-7. Write out His "I Am" statement and answer.

5 What do these questions reveal about the disciples' understanding or misunderstanding of Jesus?

WHAT DO YOU THINK?

"Jesus said to him, 'I am the way, and the truth, and the life. No one comes to the Father except through Me.'"

JOHN 14:6

The Way

6 Read the following verses and write out why Jesus is the only Way.

Hebrews 10:1-18

Acts 4:11-12

1 Timothy 2:5

7 The disciples asked Jesus twice where He was going. What is His response in John 14:2-4?

8 Read Romans 5:18-19. "Therefore, as one trespass led to condemnation for all men, so one act of righteousness leads to justification and life for all men. For as by the one man's disobedience the many were made sinners, so by the one man's obedience the many will be made righteous." With John 14:2-7 and Romans 5:18-19 as guides, explain in your own words what Jesus meant when He declared "I am the way."

The Truth

9 Read the passages provided from the Psalms. Highlight the characteristics of truth which are given about the Lord.

Psalm 18:30

This God—His way is perfect;
the word of the LORD proves
true;
He is a shield for all those who
take refuge in Him.

Psalm 119:137-144

[137]Righteous are You, O LORD,
and right are Your rules.
[138]You have appointed Your
testimonies in righteousness
and in all faithfulness.
[139]My zeal consumes me,
because my foes forget Your
words.
[140]Your promise is well tried,
and Your servant loves it.
[141]I am small and despised,
yet I do not forget Your precepts.
[142]Your righteousness is

righteous forever,
and Your law is true.
¹⁴³*Trouble and anguish have*
found me out,
but Your commandments are my
delight.
¹⁴⁴*Your testimonies are*
righteous forever;
give me understanding that I
may live.

10 With John 14:7 and the Psalms provided as guides, explain in your own words what Jesus meant when He declared "I am the truth."

The Life

Read 1 Corinthians 15:20-26.

"But in fact Christ has been raised from the dead, the first fruits of those who have fallen asleep. For as by a man came death, by a man has come also the resurrection of

199

the dead. For as in Adam all die, so also in Christ shall all be made alive. But each in his own order: Christ the first fruits, then at His coming those who belong to Christ. Then comes the end, when He delivers the kingdom to God the Father after destroying every rule and every authority and power. For He must reign until He has put all His enemies under His feet. The last enemy to be destroyed is death."

11 With John 14:3 and 1 Corinthians 15:20-26 as guides, explain in your own words what Jesus meant when He declared "I am the life."

12 Imagine a scenario where a friend or coworker who is unfamiliar with Christianity asks you to explain what you believe. Using Jesus's "I am the way, the truth, and the life" statement, formulate an answer to your friend's question.

WHAT'S IT TO YOU?
Blessed Assurance

13 Read John 14:1 and 14:27. What command did Jesus give in both verses?

14 In John 14:27 Jesus stated, "Peace I leave with you; My peace I give to you." Describe the difference between the peace of the world and the peace of the Lord.

15 Jesus used this last meal as an opportunity to encourage and offer assurance to His followers. Use the chart provided to make a list of the promises and assurances you see in Jesus's final discourse.

Jesus's Promise

JOHN
13:34; 15:9;
17:26

JOHN
14:1-3

JOHN
14:23

JOHN
14:16, 26;
15:26; 16:7

JOHN
14:18, 20-21

Jesus's Promise

JOHN
14:27

JOHN
15:11; 16:22

JOHN
15:16

JOHN
16:23

JOHN
16:33

16 Think of an area in your life where you are currently feeling troubled (e.g., a broken relationship, anxieties about a job, or your health). How can Jesus's words of assurance be applied and offer rest for your troubled heart? (Pick one or two verses from the chart to specifically apply to your situation.)

On the night of this final discourse, Jesus knew His final hours were approaching and that He was about to suffer a great sorrow. And yet the Lord's kindness and compassion are on display in these chapters as Jesus spends His time not in asking His friends to comfort Him, but in giving them assurance, comfort, and direction.

17 In closing, take some time to pray or to journal. Look back at the chart in question 15, thank the Lord for His lovingkindness in your life. Pray that His words of comfort given to the disciples 2,000 years ago would give you comfort (and confidence) as you wrestle with the brokenness of the world today.

The True Vine:
GOD'S DIVINE UNITY

"I am the true vine . . . Abide in Me, and I in you."

JOHN 15:1a, 4a

THINK ABOUT IT

Before its destruction in 70 A.D., the Jewish Temple in Jerusalem was filled with magnificent icons. Each golden lampstand, curtain, gate and pillar, offered a symbol for worshipers, reminding them of the majesty and faithfulness of their holy God. One of the symbols, described by the ancient historian Josephus was a golden vine which hung over the entrance door with "clusters of grapes hung as tall as a man's height."[5] Even today the image of the vine and the fruit it produces is as prevalent in Jewish art and culture as the cross is in Christian.

Why do you think humans respond to metaphors and images? What purpose do images, art, and stories play in the human experience? Name any pieces of art that have significant meaning to you.

WHAT DO YOU SEE?
A Loving Assurance

1 As the next chapter begins, remember John 15 is a continuation of one message which began in John 13. Take a moment to look back at a few important points already studied from Jesus's final message to His disciples.

a. After Jesus washed the disciples' feet, He gave them a command. Write out John 13:34-35.

b. What promise did Jesus give the disciples in John 14:2?

c. What reassurance did Jesus give the disciples in John 14:3?

d. What declaration and instruction did Jesus give the disciples in John 14:6?

2 Read John 14:27-31. What did Jesus say was His reason for giving the disciples this final message?

John 15:1 opens with Jesus's next identity claim: "I am the true vine and my Father is the vinedresser." Bread, light, life, and death are all a part of the collective human experience, but while Jesus's next declaration may seem somewhat outside of today's cultural norm, it had deeply rooted meaning to

His Jewish audience. Starting in Genesis (Gen. 9:20, Lev. 19:10, Amos 9:13-15) the vine is used as a symbol of the Lord's provision for Israel. But as the story unfolds, the vineyard (Israel), planted and cultivated by the vinedresser, repeatedly disregards, rebels and proves unfaithful to the Lord (Ps. 80; Isa. 5:1-7; Jer. 2:20-22; Ezek. 19:10-14; Hos. 10:1-2). Closely read a couple of these Old Testament passages. Then answer the questions that follow to connect them with John 15.

The Unfaithful Vine

Read and mark Isaiah 5:1-7.

- Circle any reference given to the vine.

- Highlight the protection the beloved provided for the vineyard.

- In another color, highlight what happened when the vineyard was unfaithful.

Isaiah 5:1-7

*¹Let me sing for my beloved
my love song concerning His
vineyard:
My beloved had a vineyard
on a very fertile hill.
²He dug it and cleared it of
stones,
 and planted it with choice*

vines;
He built a watchtower in the
midst of it,
and hewed out a wine vat in it;
and He looked for it to yield
grapes,
but it yielded wild grapes.

³"And now, O inhabitants of
Jerusalem
and men of Judah,
judge between Me and My
vineyard.
⁴What more was there to do for
My vineyard,
that I have not done in it?
When I looked for it to yield
grapes,
why did it yield wild grapes?

⁵"And now I will tell you
what I will do to My vineyard.
I will remove its hedge,
and it shall be devoured;
I will break down its wall,
and it shall be trampled down.
⁶I will make it a waste;
it shall not be pruned or hoed,
and briers and thorns shall

grow up;
I will also command the clouds
that they rain no rain upon it."
⁷For the vineyard of the LORD
of hosts
is the house of Israel,
and the men of Judah
are His pleasant planting;
and He looked for justice,
but behold, bloodshed;
for righteousness,
but behold, an outcry!

3 To whom does "my beloved" refer in 5:1?

4 Whom did Isaiah twice identify as the vineyard?

5 Isaiah 5:3-4 provides the turning point for this passage.

a. In what ways was the beloved faithful to the vineyard in 5:1-4?

b. How did the vineyard respond?

6 What was the fruit of faithfulness for which the Lord looked in Isaiah 5:7? What did He find instead?

Psalm 80 is a passage which also details Israel's unfaithfulness, but unlike Isaiah 5, Psalm 80 concludes with a cry to the Lord. Read the passage provided and answer the corresponding questions.

Psalm 80:14-19

[14]*Turn again, O God of hosts!*
Look down from heaven, and
see;
have regard for this vine,
[15]*the stock that Your right hand*
planted,
and for the son whom You made
strong for Yourself.
[16]*They have burned it with fire;*
they have cut it down;
may they perish at the rebuke of
Your face!
[17]*But let Your hand be on the*
man of Your right hand,
the son of man whom You have
made strong for Yourself!
[18]*Then we shall not turn back*
from You;
give us life, and we will call
upon Your name!
[19]*Restore us, O LORD God of*
hosts!
Let Your face shine, that we may
be saved!

7 What was the psalmist requesting of the Lord when he cried out in these verses?

8 According to Psalm 80, who can restore the vine? How?

Abiding in the Vine

Read and mark John 15:1-10.

- Underline Jesus's "I Am" statement.

- Circle the participants in the passage.

- Using different colors, highlight Jesus's commands to "abide."

- In the margins make note of how many times Jesus used the word "abide."

John 15:1-10

[1]"I am the true vine, and My Father is the vinedresser. [2]Every branch in Me that does not bear fruit He takes away, and every branch that does bear fruit He prunes, that it may bear more fruit. [3]Already you are clean because of the word that I have spoken to you. [4]Abide in Me, and I in you. As the branch cannot bear fruit by itself, unless it abides in the vine, neither can you, unless you abide in Me. [5]I am the vine; you are the branches. Whoever abides in Me and I in him, he it is that bears much fruit, for apart from Me you can do nothing. [6]If anyone does not abide in Me, he is thrown away like a branch and withers; and the branches are gathered, thrown into the fire, and burned. [7]If you abide in Me, and My words abide in you, ask whatever you wish, and it will be done for you. [8]By this My Father is glorified, that you bear much fruit and so

*prove to be My disciples. ⁹As the
Father has loved Me, so have I
loved you. Abide in My love. ¹⁰If
you keep My commandments,
you will abide in My love, just
as I have kept My Father's
commandments and abide in
His love."*

9 The word *abide*, while used frequently in the Bible, is not used commonly today. Read Psalm 91:1-2. Using the psalm as a reference, write out in your own words what it means to abide in the Lord.

10 Fill in the blanks below to help clarify what abiding in Jesus looks like.

John 15:2 – Abiding in Christ means the Lord
_____ you.

John 15:4-5 – Abiding in Christ means you bear or

produce _____.

John 15:7 – Abiding in Christ means you are rooted in His _____.

John 15:9 – Abiding in Christ means you are _____.

John 15:10 – Abiding in Christ means your desire becomes to keep the Lord's _____.

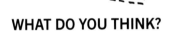

WHAT DO YOU THINK?

11 With question 10 in mind, give practical examples from your own life of what abiding in Christ from day to day looks like. Where would you like to see growth in your abiding dependence on Christ?

12 In his commentary on the book of John, John Calvin argued that John 15:5 "is the conclusion and application of the whole parable."[6]

a. Write out Jesus's proclamation in John 15:5.

b. In your own words, what does His proclamation mean?

Union with Christ

In John 15, Jesus repeatedly used the phrases "abide" and "in me." Paul and other New Testament authors continued this teaching concept with phrases such as "if anyone is in Christ" (2 Cor. 5:17) and "Christ in you" (Col. 1:27). Taking it a step further, theologians, such as the 20th century Scottish professor John Murray, have called this doctrine "union with Christ." Murray believed, "Nothing is more central or basic [in the Christian life] than union and communion with Christ . . .

Union with Christ is really the central truth of the whole doctrine of salvation."[7] Simply stated, for Christians, Christ's nature becomes our identity and Christ Himself is our home (Ps. 17:6-9, Ps. 91). (See Appendix C.)

13 Across time believers have needed to be reminded often of the fundamental truth of God's love and commitment to His people. Paul knew this and desired for his brothers and sisters in the church of Ephesus to remember the joy, confidence, and righteousness that was theirs through their union with Christ. Read Ephesians 2:4-8, and then answer the questions.

a. Ephesians 2:4-6 – Why did God make "us alive together with Christ"?

b. Ephesians 2:6 – Where do you see "union with Christ" applied in this verse?

c. Ephesians 2:7 – How do we have access to God's grace and kindness?

d. What similar teaching is found in both Ephesians 2:8 and John 15:5?

WHAT'S IT TO YOU?

14 Being united with Christ means that your identity is first and foremost in Christ. Does the idea of union with Christ encourage or threaten you? What do you feel you are gaining, or maybe losing, when your identity is defined by your union with Christ?

15 Today's society places a high value on personal independence, but Jesus and Paul both taught that the core of Christianity is dependence on Christ alone. Name a few places where personal independence has shaped your worldview. Then name how Jesus's commands in John 15, to abide in Him, affirm or challenge your worldview.

16 In the next chapter we will look more closely at the roles of the vine, the vinedresser, and the branches, but for now, look back at question 10. The statements in this question are reflections of a life united to and abiding in Christ. From which of these statements do you feel the most disconnected? How can your union with Christ bring you comfort when you have those feelings of disconnection?

17 In closing, write out John 15:9, taking time to reflect on the beautiful truth of the passage. Let Jesus's words remind you of the deep love the Father, Son, and Holy Spirit have for you. Write out a prayer asking the Lord to help you abide with Him in specific places and to help you grow in dependence on the nourishment of the True Vine.

The True Vine:
ABIDING IN OUR TRUE HOME

"I am the true vine . . . Abide in Me, and I in you."

JOHN 15:1, 4

THINK ABOUT IT

"Sanctification through union with Christ, however, does not mean that we lose our individuality. Rather, it means that our gifts and abilities are progressively honed, developed, and purified so that we become our best selves."[8]

Union with Christ means that Christ's character becomes our core identity, though we maintain our individuality as God's unique creations. How can having a firm foundation in your Christ-centered identity free you to be the individual God has uniquely made you to be?

Faith and Fellowship

Jesus's care and compassion for His followers was on full display in His final discourse. Jesus wanted His disciples (and His followers for years to come) to fully understand who He is and the role He has played in God's redemptive plan, and to equip them for the challenges they would face. Jesus knew His next few days would be filled with deep sorrow (John 19), but His main concern was in caring for His beloved followers. He showed compassion with a physical example of His love (John 13:1-12); He petitioned for their faith (John 13:19; 14:1, 7, 11; 16:4); and finally He revealed the depth of their union with Him (John 14:16-17; 15:9, 15; 16:33). Using both a passionate plea and a compassionate pledge, Jesus invited His followers throughout the ages to abide with Him in an eternal fellowship.

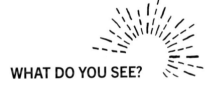

WHAT DO YOU SEE?

Read and mark John 15:1-17.

- Underline Jesus's "I Am" statement.

- In different colors highlight each place the Father, Jesus, or the branch are discussed.

- In another color, highlight how the Father is glorified.

- Using yet another color, highlight the pruning work of the vinedresser towards the branch.

John 15:1-17

[1]*"I am the true vine, and My Father is the vinedresser.* [2]*Every branch in Me that does not bear fruit He takes away, and every branch that does bear fruit He prunes, that it may bear more fruit.* [3]*Already you are clean because of the word that I have spoken to you.* [4]*Abide in Me, and I in you. As the branch cannot bear fruit by itself, unless it abides in the vine, neither can you, unless you abide in Me.* [5]*I am the vine; you are the branches. Whoever abides in Me and I in him, he it is that bears much fruit, for apart from Me you can do nothing.* [6]*If anyone does not abide in Me, he is thrown away like a branch and withers; and the branches are gathered, thrown into the fire, and burned.* [7]*If you abide in Me, and My words abide in you, ask whatever you wish, and it will be done for you.* [8]*By this My Father is glorified, that you bear much fruit and so*

prove to be My disciples. ⁹As the
Father has loved Me, so have I
loved you. Abide in My love. ¹⁰If
you keep My commandments,
you will abide in My love, just
as I have kept my Father's
commandments and abide in
His love. ¹¹These things I have
spoken to you, that My joy may
be in you, and that your joy may
be full.

¹²"This is My commandment,
that you love one another as
I have loved you. ¹³Greater
love has no one than this, that
someone lay down his life for
his friends. ¹⁴You are My friends
if you do what I command
you. ¹⁵No longer do I call you
servants, for the servant does
not know what his master is
doing; but I have called you
friends, for all that I have heard
from My Father I have made
known to you. ¹⁶You did not
choose Me, but I chose you and
appointed you that you should
go and bear fruit and that your

fruit should abide, so that
whatever you ask the Father
in My name, He may give it to
you. *[17]These things I command*
you, so that you will love one
another.

1 Through the use of metaphor, Jesus identified three roles in this passage. For each role given, answer the following questions: Who fulfills the role? What are the responsibilities of the role?

The Vinedresser:

The Vine:

The Branch:

The Pruning Work of the Vinedresser

2 Jesus identified His Father as the Vinedresser who disciples and disciplines. Read the two passages provided in the chart to gain a further understanding of the Father's pruning work in His people. For each passage, answer the following questions:

a. Who does the Father prune?
b. Why does the Father prune His people?
c. How does the Father prune them?

	a.
PROVERBS 3:11-12	b.
	c.

231

HEBREWS
12:7-11

a.

b.

c.

Pruning is done by gardeners to promote healthy growth in their plants. In the same way, the Divine Gardener, the Vinedresser, prunes to promote healthy growth in His people. This transforming work is known as sanctification.

3 Read 2 Corinthians 3:16-18. Paul taught that those who trust in the Lord are transformed. What are they transformed (sanctified) into?

4 Read 1 Corinthians 1:30-31. With these verses and the lesson from chapter 12 (particularly Eph. 2:4-6) in mind, how are we transformed (sanctified)?

The Fruit of the Branches

5 Go back to the John 15 passage printed at the beginning of this lesson.

a. Underline each time Jesus used the word "fruit." How many times is it used?

b. List the fruit Jesus wants to produce in His children.

John 15:9 –

John 15:11 –

John 15:12 –

John 15:17 –

John 16:33 –

6 A merit-based society trains its members to believe that good things ("the fruit" of life) come only from an individual's hard work. But this is not the case in God's economy. In John 15:4-5, how did Jesus say the branches produce fruit?

7 Throughout His message Jesus promised that when He departed, His followers would not be left alone. Who did Jesus promise would be an aide for His followers in John 14:16-17, 25-26?

8 What is one of the roles of the Helper that Jesus identified in John 15:26?

9 The apostle Paul also talked about the fruit of life produced from abiding in the Lord. In Galatians 5:16 and 25, who did Paul say produces fruit in believers?

10 List the fruit Paul named in Galatians 5:22-23.

WHAT DO YOU THINK?

11 Imagine you are leading a discussion on this passage and someone has asked you to explain the Vinedresser. Use only one or two sentences to explain the identity and work of the Vinedresser.

12 What command did Jesus repeat in John 13:34-35; 15:12 and 17?

13 Drawing on what you have learned over the course of this study, why did Jesus consider this command to be of such importance?

14 Who are some people in your life who have lived out this command well? What are some things you would like to learn from them? If you know their story, what pruning did they undergo that has added in the formation of their Christian character? (Consider asking them!)

WHAT'S IT TO YOU?

John 15:6 is not a full doctrine of election or salvation. Scripture repeatedly states that those who are in the Lord will remain in the Lord (Rom. 8:28-39, Phil. 1:6, 1 John 2:19-25). Here, in the context of His whole message and the whole book of John, Jesus was giving a watchful warning. He cautioned His followers that some branches may seem green for a season, but they will wither after a time (Judas would be an example. See John 12:6; 13:2, 27). Only those who humbly depend on the Vine are nourished and sustained by the Vine.

15 In context with the rest of John 15, verse 6 leads the readers to evaluate their own lives. How have you abided in the Vine? How have you found your true home in Him? List ways He has sustained and sanctified you through the true and faithful Vine.

16 How have you experienced the Father's pruning work in your life? What did it feel like when you were in the middle of that experience? Looking back now, where do you see growth in your spiritual maturity because of the Father's pruning work through that experience(s)?

17 The purpose of the Father's pruning is to grow and sanctify His children into the likeness of Christ. Where in your current life could you benefit from the Father's loving act of pruning?

18 The two lists of fruit in questions 4 and 9, originally from Jesus in John 15 and Paul in Galatians 5, are a helpful diagnostic list. When you are abiding in Jesus Christ, you are learning, growing, and actively being sanctified—even if it is in small ways. What fruit have you seen being produced in your current life circumstances or from your past experiences?

19 In closing, take some time to read and meditate on John 15:10-11. The fruit produced in your life does not unite you to Christ, but it is a beautiful overflow of the reality of who you are: one with Christ. Jesus knew the dark days the disciples were going to face after His departure, and He wanted them to fully understand how deeply He loved them. Jesus also knows every dark moment you have faced and wants you to grasp just how deeply He delights in you. Jesus was obedient to the commands of the Father, overcoming the darkness of this world, because of His love for you. Your new identity is now found in one whose joy is *in* you and whose joy is in *you* . . . forever. Write out a prayer that His joy, peace, and faithfulness would be deeply rooted in you moment by moment.

The Alpha and the Omega:
THE COVENANT MAKER AND KEEPER

"I am the Alpha and the Omega, the first and the last, the beginning and the end."

REVELATION 22:13

THINK ABOUT IT

After Jesus finished His final discourse, He prayed to the Father; then He was arrested, beaten, and crucified. The contrast between the comforting dinner amongst friends and Jesus's horrific death must have been stark for His disciples. It can be tempting to see those men and women as cowards, but think of a time you felt confident only to have your confidence unexpectedly dashed. How do you deal with your confusion or anger when things in your life are not going the way it seems the Lord promised they would?

In chapters 18-19, John gave His account of Jesus's crucifixion and death. But praise be to God, as promised, on the third day Jesus's dead heart began to beat again, His eyes reopened, the Son of God stood up and walked out of His burial tomb (John 20). Just as John the Baptist and the prophets before Him had foretold, Jesus the Lamb of God had taken away the sin of the world and conquered the power of death forevermore (John 1:29).

The apostle John also wrote four other New Testament books: 1, 2, and 3 John and Revelation. Revelation can seem to be an overwhelming book, but at its core, it is a story of God's greatness and power. No evil can overcome Him—God is going to win! And in the midst of this story, we find Jesus giving another important identity claim.

WHAT DO YOU SEE?
The First and Last "I AM"

Read and mark the following passages.

- Highlight Jesus's "I Am" statements.

- In another color, highlight Jesus's divinity claim.

- Circle the actions of God.

- In the margins, connect any descriptions with Jesus's other "I Am" statements.

Revelation 1:1-8

¹The revelation of Jesus Christ, which God gave Him to show to His servants the things that must soon take place. He made it known by sending His angel to His servant John, ²who bore witness to the word of God and to the testimony of Jesus Christ, even to all that he saw. ³Blessed is the one who reads aloud the words of this prophecy, and blessed are those who hear, and who keep what is written in it, for the time is near.

⁴John to the seven churches that are in Asia:

Grace to you and peace from Him Who is and Who was and Who is to come, and from the seven spirits who are before His throne, ⁵and from Jesus Christ the faithful witness, the firstborn of the dead, and the ruler of kings on earth. To Him who loves us and has freed us from our sins by His blood ⁶and

made us a kingdom, priests
to His God and Father, to Him
be glory and dominion forever
and ever. Amen. ⁷Behold, He is
coming with the clouds, and
every eye will see Him, even
those who pierced Him, and all
tribes of the earth will wail on
account of Him. Even so. Amen.

⁸"I am the Alpha and the
Omega," says the Lord God,
"Who is and Who was and Who
is to come, the Almighty."

Revelation 21:1-7

¹Then I saw a new heaven and a
new earth, for the first heaven
and the first earth had passed
away, and the sea was no more.
²And I saw the holy city, new
Jerusalem, coming down out of
heaven from God, prepared as a
bride adorned for her husband.
³And I heard a loud voice from
the throne saying, "Behold, the
dwelling place of God is with
man. He will dwell with them,
and they will be His people, and

God Himself will be with them
as their God. ⁴He will wipe away
every tear from their eyes, and
death shall be no more, neither
shall there be mourning, nor
crying, nor pain anymore, for
the former things have passed
away."

⁵And He who was seated on
the throne said, "Behold, I am
making all things new." Also
He said, "Write this down, for
these words are trustworthy
and true." ⁶And He said to me,
"It is done! I am the Alpha and
the Omega, the beginning and
the end. To the thirsty I will give
from the spring of the water of
life without payment. ⁷The one
who conquers will have this
heritage, and I will be his God
and he will be My son.

Revelation 22:13

"I am the Alpha and the Omega,
the first and the last, the
beginning and the end."

1 To whom was Revelation written?

2 List the descriptions of Jesus given in Revelation 1:5-8.

3 Read Exodus 25:8-9. According to Exodus 25:8-9 and Revelation 21:3, where does God want to dwell?

4 From Genesis to Revelation the whole Bible is proclaiming the Lord's covenant promise of salvation and restoration of His family.

a. How does Revelation 1:5-6 describe Jesus's faithful obedience?

b. Through Jesus's obedience God's promises are now the inheritance of His children. List the blessings of that inheritance given in Revelation 21:1-7.

WHAT DO YOU THINK?

5 The Lord identifies Himself as the Alpha and Omega three times in Revelation. Alpha and omega are the first and last letters of the Greek alphabet. But even if you didn't know that, Jesus gives two direct explanations in Revelation 21:6 and 22:13. What did Jesus mean when He said He is the Alpha and Omega?

6 Write out other Bible passages which declare God's eternal nature (For example: Lam. 3:19-24, Job 36:26, Ps. 93:1-2).

Isaiah's Encouragement

Read and mark Isaiah 43:1-3a, 10-13.

- Underline any identity statements made.
- Highlight the promises of the Lord.
- In another color highlight the commands given to the Lord's people.
- In the margins write the similarities you see with the passages already marked in this chapter.

Isaiah 43:1-3a, 10-13

¹*But now thus says the LORD,*
He who created you, O Jacob,
He who formed you, O Israel:
"Fear not, for I have redeemed you;
I have called you by name, you are Mine.
²*When you pass through the waters, I will be with you;*
and through the rivers, they shall not overwhelm you;
when you walk through fire you shall not be burned,
and the flame shall not consume you.
³*For I am the LORD your God,*
the Holy One of Israel, your

252

Savior.

[10]"You are My witnesses,"
declares the LORD,
"and My servant whom I have
chosen,
that you may know and believe
Me
and understand that I am He.
Before Me no god was formed,
nor shall there be any after Me.
[11]I, I am the LORD,
and besides Me there is no
savior.
[12]I declared and saved and
proclaimed,
when there was no strange god
among you;
and you are My witnesses,"
declares the LORD, "and I am
God.
[13]Also henceforth I am He;
there is none who can deliver
from My hand;
I work, and who can turn it
back?"

Isaiah was written to the Lord's people during a time when a majority had turned away from worshiping their covenant Redeemer. God loves His people and is jealous for their affection. Isaiah wrote to remind God's people of their identity, to call them to repentance, and to lead them back to worshiping their one true Father.

7 List at least three ways God provided for the Israelites as recorded in Isaiah 43.

8 Name two identity claims children of God can make based on Isaiah 43.

9 Read Deuteronomy 33:27. How did Moses identify God in this passage?

10 Turn again to the beginning of John. How was Jesus identified in John 1:1-3?

11 Looking back at the passages read this week, how did the authors of Deuteronomy 33:27; Isaiah 43; John 1; and Revelation 1, 21, and 22 all identify the Lord?

12 Throughout the Bible the Lord is described as eternal and everlasting. What importance does the Lord's everlasting nature hold? (Think both of what it means for you personally and for the whole of the world).

WHAT'S IT TO YOU?
God's Unchanging Identity

13 Jesus's final discourse in John chapters 13-17, was full of direction and hope which concluded teaching with a powerful declaration. Write out John 16:33.

14 What are some similarities between Jesus's statement to the disciples in John 16:33 and in the Revelation passages provided above?

15 What comfort, confusion, or confidence do Jesus's words in John 16:33 give you?

16 Once you are united with Christ as a beloved child of God, you are always a beloved child of God. While your core identity does not change, you are given a unique role, personality, and story that are being developed over the course of your life.

a. Name some of the roles, relationships, and/or experiences that make you unique.

b. Your identity in Christ, the Alpha and the Omega, affects every part of your life. Look back at the list you just made, where in your story do you struggle to believe that identity is true?

c. List some passages you know that can help you live out your identity in Christ. Consider taking the time to memorize one or two, so they are always available to you when you need them.

17 Think about a place in your own life where you feel exhausted, hurt, or maybe even hopeless. Look back at the Revelation passages given at the beginning of the lesson. What promises does the Lord give in those verses? How do those promises provide hope in your situation?

Close in prayer, remembering Jesus's declaration to the disciples (and you!):

> *"I have said these things to you, that in Me you may have peace. In the world you will have tribulation. But take heart; I have overcome the world."*

JOHN 16:33

CONCLUSION

As you conclude this study, use the questions provided as a guide to help you reflect over what you have learned.

a. How has the study of Jesus's "I Am" statements changed or expanded your view of who God is?

b. How does God's identity affect the identity of every believer?

c. Name one or two ways studying the "I Am" statements of Jesus has changed your view of yourself.

"In the beginning was the Word, and the Word was with God, and the Word was God. He was in the beginning with God. All things were made through Him, and without Him was not any thing made that was made. In Him was life, and the life was the light of men. The light shines in the darkness, and the darkness has not overcome it."

JOHN 1:1-5

The appendices on the following pages are included to help you take your work in this study a step further.

Appendix A
JESUS'S "I AM" STATEMENTS

As you work through the study, use this chart to keep track of the importance of each "I Am" statement.

Jesus's "I Am" Statement	Who is Christ Jesus?
The Bread of Life JOHN 6:47-48	
The Light of the World JOHN 8:12	
The Door and the Good Shepherd JOHN 10:9, 11	

Jesus's "I Am" Statement	Who is Christ Jesus?
The Resurrection and the Life JOHN 11:25	
The Way, the Truth and the Life JOHN 14:1a, 6	
The True Vine JOHN 15:1	
The Alpha and the Omega REVELATION 1:8 and 21:6	

Appendix B
COVENANT THEOLOGY

"I will take you to be My people, and I will be your God, and you shall know that I am the LORD your God"

EXODUS 6:7a

A covenant is an agreement made between two or more parties. In the Bible the overarching story of God's redemptive plan is highlighted in the covenants God makes between Himself and mankind. But God, understanding the depths of the sinfulness of mankind, knows that ultimately in each covenant, He will have to fulfill both sides of the agreement. God demands payment for the brokenness of this world, but in His mercy, through His Son, He pays the penalty for His people.

Use the following chart to review the covenants made between God and His people.

THE COVENANT WITH CREATION

	GENESIS 1-3	HOSEA 6:7
Covenant Story		
Who was involved in the covenant?		
What covenant promise was made?		
Name two things this covenant reveals about the Lord.		

THE COVENANT WITH NOAH

GENESIS
9:8-17

Covenant
Story

Who was
involved
in the
covenant?

What
covenant
promise was
made?

Name two
things this
covenant
reveals
about the
Lord.

THE COVENANT WITH ABRAHAM

GENESIS
12:1-3

Covenant
Story

Who was
involved
in the
covenant?

What
covenant
promise was
made?

Name two
things this
covenant
reveals
about the
Lord.

THE COVENANT WITH MOSES

EXODUS
19:3-6

Covenant Story	
Who was involved in the covenant?	
What covenant promise was made?	
Name two things this covenant reveals about the Lord.	

THE COVENANT WITH DAVID

2 SAMUEL
7:8-16

Covenant
Story

Who was
involved
in the
covenant?

What
covenant
promise was
made?

Name two
things this
covenant
reveals
about the
Lord.

THE NEW COVENANT

	JEREMIAH 31:31-34	1 CORINTHIANS 11:23-26
Covenant Story		
Who was involved in the covenant?		
What covenant promise was made?		
Name two things this covenant reveals about the Lord.		

271

Appendix C
UNION WITH CHRIST

"I have been crucified with Christ. It is no longer I who live, but Christ who lives in me. And the life I now live in the flesh I live by faith in the Son of God, who loved me and gave Himself for me."

GALATIANS 2:20

Union with Christ can be described as the core component of the Christian faith. Through the continual, uniting work of the Holy Spirit, Christ is in His followers and His followers are in Christ (Gal. 2:19-20). In John 15, Jesus explained union with Christ through the imagery of the vine. Christ is the vine, the life and bloodline of His followers, the branches. To enrich your understanding, use the chart provided to review other places in Scripture where union with Christ is explained.

Union with Christ Passage	What is your new identity provided through your union with Christ?
ROMANS 5	

Union with Christ Passage	What is your new identity provided through your union with Christ?
1 JOHN 4:13-19	
ROMANS 8:1-11	
COLOSSIANS 3:9-10	

Endnotes

1   John Calvin, *Institutes of the Christian Religion*. Edited by John T. McNeil. (Philadelphia: The Westminster Press, 1960), 35, 39.

2   From Genesis to Revelation the whole Bible tells the story of God fulfilling His covenant promise of salvation, of the restoration of His people. For a review of God's covenants with His people. See Appendix B.

3   John Calvin, *Commentary on Gospel of John*. Edited by Alister McGrath and J.I. Packer. (Wheaton, IL: Crossway Books, 1994), 13.

4   Joni Eareckson Tada. *The God I Love: A Lifetime Walking with Jesus*. (Grand Rapids, MI: Zondervan, 2003).

5   Flavius Josephus, "Description of the Jerusalem Temple," *War of the Jews, Book 5*. Found on https://www.fisheaters.com/temple.html.

6   John Calvin, *Commentary on Gospel of John*. Edited by Alister McGrath and J.I. Packer. (Wheaton, IL: Crossway Books, 1994), 354.

7   John Murray, *Redemption Accomplished and Applied*. (Grand Rapids: Wm. B. Eerdmans Publishing Co., 1955), 161.

8   Anthony Hoekema, *Saved by Grace*. (Grand Rapids:Wm. B. Eerdmans Publishing Co., 1989), 62.

Other Resources

Colin G. Kruse, *John, Tyndale New Testament Commentaries, Vol. 4.* (Downers Grove, IL: InterVarsity Press, 2003).

Robert W. Yarbrough, *John.* (Chicago: Moody Press, 1991).